Rhetoric
in the New World

Studies in Rhetoric/Communication

Thomas W. Benson, General Editor

Rhetoric in the New World

Rhetorical Theory and Practice in Colonial Spanish America

Don Paul Abbott

UNIVERSITY OF SOUTH CAROLINA PRESS

Grateful acknowledgment is made to the Program for Cultural
Cooperation Between Spain's Ministry of Culture and United States'
Universities for their financial support of this project.

Copyright © 1996 University of South Carolina

Published in Columbia, South Carolina, by the
University of South Carolina Press

Manufactured in the United States of America

00 99 98 97 96   5 4 3 2 1

Library of Congress Cataloging-in-Publication Data

Abbott, Don Paul, 1947–
    Rhetoric in the New World : rhetorical theory and practice in
colonial Spanish America / Don Paul Abbott.
        p.   cm. —(Studies in rhetoric/communication)
    Includes bibliographical references and index.
    ISBN 1–57003–085-5
    1. Spanish language —Rhetoric. 2. Spanish American prose
literature—To 1800—History and criticism. 3. Rhetoric—Latin
America. 4. Persuasion (Rhetoric) 5. Preaching—Latin America.
I. Title II. Series.
PC4410.A33 1996
808'.0461—dc20   95–41775

To Elizabeth
without whom not

Kenneth Burke
A Grammar of Motives

Contents

Illustrations

General Editor's Preface

In *Rhetoric in the New World*, Don Paul Abbott explores rhetorical theories of the sixteenth and seventeenth centuries in Spain's American empire. The Columbian encounter and Spain's colonization of empires in New Spain and Peru came at a time when the study of rhetoric, based on newly discovered classical texts, was a central subject in Renaissance humanism. Spain's efforts to colonize, subordinate, govern, and educate its New World subjects were executed with armed force and persuasion. A central feature of Spanish expansion was the effort to convert indigenous populations to the Catholic faith, an effort that influenced conceptions of rhetorical theory. The rediscovery of classical rhetoric had initiated in Europe a revision of medieval rhetorical doctrines. Would that new European rhetoric be judged suitable to the task of evangelizing the American colonies, or would it, in its turn, need to be adapted to an alien context? Abbott traces the various answers to this question through the work of a remarkable series of rhetorical theorists.

Luis de Granada (1504–88), himself a famous preacher, wrote two treatises on preaching, one addressed to converting peoples of the East and West Indies, the other to preaching to the already Christian peoples of Europe. These audiences, in Granada's view, required rhetoric based on classical precepts but variously adapted to their particular conditions. Granada's *Ecclesiasticae rhetoricae*, which propounded a rhetoric suitable to European Christians, assumes that the audience needed preaching that would intensify its commitment to the faith by converting it to Christian action—hence, Granada devotes considerable attention to amplification as a means to arouse emotion. In contrast, the *Breve tratado*, describing a rhetoric for newly encountered non-Christians, assumes that, as humans, these audiences are rational, but that, not having been exposed to Christianity, they require brief and rational appeals to belief.

Bernardino de Sahagún, a Franciscan friar who arrived in the New World in 1529, collected in the original Nahuatl language a large number of traditional orations recalled from the pre-Columbian time; these orations were reported in book six of Sahagún's *The General History of New Spain*. Sahagún's collection permits a glimpse of a highly developed rhetorical culture that was destroyed by colonization.

Diego Valadés, a mestizo born in the New World, was one of very few non-Europeans admitted to the clergy before the synod of 1555 prohibited the practice. In his *Rhetorica Christiana*, Valadés, trained by the Franciscans in Ciceronian rhetoric, argues that rhetorical education is the key to bringing Christianity and civilization to the New World. Whereas earlier scholars have sometimes viewed the *Rhetorica Christiana* as a disorganized mixture of classical rhetoric with observations about the peoples of Mexica, Abbott argues that when the two themes are interpreted from a truly rhetorical perspective, they resolve into a well-organized whole in which classical rhetoric confronts the culture of the New World.

Abbott next contrasts the views of two missionaries to the New World—Bartolomé de Las Casas and José de Acosta. Las Casas argues that there is but one way to bring any person to the Christian faith—the way of peaceful and rational appeal through the means of classical rhetoric. Acosta, on the other hand, argues that native peoples are often significantly different from one another and hence must be appealed to with different rhetorics, including, for some, the compulsion of military force.

Whereas Diego Valadés saw himself as a European missionary to the native population, Garcilaso de la Vega, also the New World son of a Spanish father and a native mother, saw himself "as a mestizo missionary to the land of his father." In a series of works, Garcilaso argued that the central mission of bringing Christianity to the New World should be based on an understanding of the dignity, wisdom, and eloquence of the native peoples.

The divided conception of rhetoric—one for the New World, one for the Old—persisted and was once again transformed in the works of José de Arriaga. Arriaga's *Rhetoris Christiani* (1619) was a textbook on classical rhetoric for mostly Spanish students at Jesuit colleges in Peru. Arriaga's *Extirpación de la idolotría en el Perú*, while also rhetorical, describes a form of preaching designed as part of an authoritarian campaign to "extirpate" all vestiges of native religion in Peru.

Abbott's book invites readers to reconsider these rhetorics of the New World and by implication to reconsider for ourselves the way rhetorical theory and practice respond to cultural difference.

Thomas W. Benson

Acknowledgments

I owe intellectual debts to far more scholars than I can adequately acknowledge here. I can only hope that the extent of my indebtedness is made clear by the notes and bibliography. My colleague James J. Murphy has been both a source of encouragement and an invaluable resource on all matters regarding the history of rhetoric. George Kennedy of the University of North Carolina, Chapel Hill, made useful suggestions regarding chapter 2. Michael Leff of Northwestern University and Edward George of Texas Tech University both read the manuscript in its entirety and made many valuable comments and corrections. I am grateful for their efforts on behalf of my work.

I appreciate the financial support of the Committee on Research, University of California at Davis, which made possible my travel to archives to examine rare materials necessary in the preparation of this book. I am grateful also to the Program for Cultural Cooperation Between Spain's Ministry of Culture and United States' Universities for their financial support of the publication of this project.

An earlier version of chapter 2 appeared in *Rhetorica* 5 (1987): 251–64. I thank the University of California Press and the International Society for the History of Rhetoric for permission to republish. Chapter 3 first appeared in a somewhat different form in *Rhetoric and Pedagogy: Its History, Philosophy, and Practice*. My thanks to the publisher, Lawrence Earlbaum Associates, for allowing me to use it here. Illustrations from Diego Valadés's *Rhetorica Christiana* are reproduced courtesy of the Bancroft Library, University of California at Berkeley.

Finally, I want to express special gratitude to my wife, Beth, who took time out from her own hectic career to provide constant encouragement and editorial assistance. I value her support more than I can say.

Rhetoric
in the New World

Introduction

The Columbian encounter of 1492 coincided with the beginnings of a revival of the ancient art of rhetoric in Europe. Columbus's voyage had been preceded by another "discovery" that, while perhaps less dramatic, was to be of great significance for European intellectual development. In 1416 Poggio Bracciolini located a complete text of the *Institutio oratoria* by the Roman rhetorician Quintilian. Poggio's recovery of the *Institutio oratoria* made accessible once again a text that had long been available only in the most incomplete form. The consequences of these two fifteenth-century "discoveries" by Poggio and Columbus would ultimately intersect in the sixteenth century as Europeans began to transmit the ancient art of rhetoric to newly encountered worlds.

The recovery of ancient texts by Poggio and other European "book-hunters" contributed to the great Renaissance renewal of classical rhetoric. From its conceptual origins in ancient Athens rhetoric had occupied a central place in Western culture. The disintegration of the Roman Empire, however, had deprived Europe of many of the essential classical rhetorical texts. Inevitably, the medieval conception of rhetoric was shaped by this partial inheritance from antiquity. The restoration of fundamental texts such as the *Institutio oratoria* and Cicero's *De oratore* required a reevaluation of prevailing interpretations of rhetoric. This reconsideration, already under way in the fifteenth century, would continue, and indeed accelerate, in the sixteenth. Ancient rhetoric, restored and revalued by Renaissance thinkers, came to exercise enormous influence in the early modern age. It is possible that rhetoric was perhaps more widely influential in the Renaissance than at any time since its inception in ancient Athens. Rhetoric dominated the educational curriculum, guided poetic and literary creation, and provoked theological and philosophical debates.

The centrality of this discipline in the Renaissance ensured that, as Europe expanded, so too would the province of rhetoric. Yet the arrival of rhetoric in the Americas remains one of the least studied aspects of this ancient discipline's long history. It is not so much that rhetoric's role in Spain's American empire has been ignored as that it has been obscured by inquiries into other aspects of the history of European expansion.

An adequate appreciation of rhetoric in Renaissance Europe requires knowledge of a prodigious variety of philosophical, pedagogical, literary, and theological issues. The problem of scope is magnified in the New World, where rhetoric intermingled with evangelization, imperialism, anthropology, and ethnography. One consequence of this intellectual intermingling is that the examination of rhetoric in the New World has often been subordinated to other concerns. This is especially true of rhetoric's role in the Spanish campaign to convert indigenous peoples to Christianity. Yet rhetoric, the ancient art of persuasion, provided a rationale and a direction for accomplishing this enormous evangelical endeavor.

Evangelization, like all persuasive projects, must be accomplished by means of language. Nowhere was the complexity and fragility of language more apparent than in the New World, with its spectrum of symbol systems. Thus, modern scholars of the Spanish colonial experience have had to address problems of orality, literacy, translation, representation, and symbolization. Although not always recognized as such, these problems are fundamentally rhetorical.

Rhetoric was not at the margins of Renaissance thought, nor was it at the margins of the New World experience. Rhetoric was central to many aspects of the European encounter with new peoples and places, and therefore the subject of rhetoric in the New World is one of complexity and variety. I have attempted to provide an introduction to the basic issues that the rhetoricians of the Old World confronted as they struggled to comprehend the New. Although the New World encompassed virtually all of the Western Hemisphere, my concern is with the efforts of rhetoricians in Spain and its empire in the Americas. My intent is to reconstruct rhetoric's role in Spain's two great colonies, New Spain (Mexico) and Peru, territories that extended far beyond the present boundaries of the nations that bear their names. This reconstruction extends from the beginnings of Spanish colonization in the early sixteenth century to its consolidation in the seventeenth century. I have also elected to emphasize rhetorical theory, examining preceptive works that posit explicitly how human communication should be achieved. Rhetoric, however, encompasses both the theory and the practice of human expression. In the New World, very much as it had long done in Europe, rhetoric would help shape the creation of important literary works.

In chapter 1 I consider the European context for the study that follows. I have not thought it essential to chart the entire course of Spanish Renaissance rhetoric. Rather, I have chosen the work of Luis de Granada as representative of many of the issues that are important to this study. Granada is especially instructive because he is one of a handful of Spaniards who wrote both a traditional Ciceronian rhetoric and a treatise for the conversion of the natives of Asia and America. Granada's conversion manual, the *Breve tratado*, is one of the first attempts by a European to create a rhetoric directed to a non-European audience. That Granada felt it necessary to write two rather different works reveals a tension between fidelity to rhetorical traditions and the exigencies of the New World. Implicit, at least, in Granada's rhetorical works are many of the questions this study attempts to answer. In particular, I will examine whether and how Spanish rhetoricians attempted to alter or adjust ancient concepts to accommodate the New World.

In chapter 2 I document the unprecedented attempts by Europeans to preserve and analyze the preconquest discourse of Mexico. The Franciscan missionaries, especially Bernardino de Sahagún in his *General History of the Things of New Spain,* collected instances of the discourse of the Aztec, or more precisely, Mexica people. These speeches, the *huehuehtlahtolli,* the "ancient word" or the "speeches of the ancients," represents one of the very few records of the oratory of an indigenous people at the time of their early contact with Europeans. As such, the ancient word provides an invaluable record of the pervasiveness of rhetoric in Mexica society as well as a glimpse into the public discourse of a non-European people.

In chapter 3 I consider the singular career of Diego Valadés. Valadés, born in Mexico to a native mother and a Spanish father, and educated there by the Franciscans, wrote what can reasonably be called the first American rhetoric. His work, the *Rhetorica Christiana,* initiates the attempt to create a rhetoric that reflects both the Old World and the New. Although the *Rhetorica Christiana* is thoroughly within the European tradition, Valadés nevertheless modified traditional doctrine as a result of his New World experience. His life among the peoples of Mexico led

Valadés to develop a theory of rhetoric which elevates memory and graphic imagery in a manner virtually unique among Renaissance rhetorical treatises.

Chapter 4 examines the work of two missionaries, José de Acosta and Bartolomé de las Casas. In their efforts to convert the New World's natives both were forced to develop conceptions of the indigenous peoples and to construct theories of preaching consistent with these conceptions. Thus, Acosta and Las Casas confronted the question of audience in ways that European theorists had not done. Las Casas believed that the natives are human beings and thus that the precepts of rhetoric are fully applicable to them without significant alteration. In contrast, Acosta regarded the Indians as inferior to Europeans, and thus, because of this diminished capacity, rhetoric in the European tradition simply cannot work. Acosta and Las Casas reflect a fundamental division of Spanish attitudes toward indigenous peoples and how those attitudes determine alternate visions of rhetoric.

In Chapter 5 I proceed from the sixteenth to the seventeenth century and consider how rhetorical pedagogy and practice, once established in the New World, would influence the creation of colonial discourse. The effect of rhetoric on Peruvian literature is most clearly seen in the work of a mestizo, "the Inca," Garcilaso de la Vega. Garcilaso's *Royal Commentaries of the Incas,* a document directed to the Spanish Crown, employs the themes and techniques of classical rhetoric in an effort to influence Spanish colonial policy in Peru. An undertaking similar to Garcilaso's is Felipe Guaman Poma de Ayala's *Nueva corónica y buen gobierno.* Guaman Poma, an Indian influenced by Spanish sermons and missionary literature, attempted to employ these techniques on behalf of his people. Garcilaso and Guaman Poma reveal how important rhetoric had become as an instrument of intercultural communication in colonial Peru.

In the sixth and concluding chapter I continue to chart the course of rhetoric in seventeenth-century America. I begin with a consideration of José de Arriaga's *Rhetoris Christiani* and his *Extirpación de la idolatria en Peru.* The first of these books is a traditional European rhetoric, while the second is a guide for missionaries who would induce the Andeans to abandon their traditional religion. While both books are about rhetoric, they are remarkably different from one another. Arriaga's two works reflect the dichotomization of rhetoric which had occurred by the middle of the seventeenth century. Classical rhetoric had become an academic discipline suitable only for the sons of Spaniards and devoted to the replication and perpetuation of European culture in New Spain and Peru. Oratory was no longer an appropriate course for natives and mestizos; rhetorical precepts were deemed useful for purposes of conversion, but the native audience required only the most abbreviated and simplified techniques. It is this divided version of rhetoric which ultimately triumphed in the New World.

The history of rhetoric in Renaissance Europe is a subject of considerable complexity, which has justly received significant scholarly scrutiny. The course of rhetoric in the larger world beyond the boundaries of Europe, however, has been accorded considerably less attention by historians of rhetoric. Yet the rhetoricians of the New World confronted issues unanticipated by their classical predecessors and for which European experiences offered few insights. Spain's American empire was the site of extraordinary conflicts between cultures, traditions, religions, and languages. These conflicts infuse colonial rhetoric with an urgency and intricacy that often surpasses the academic contentiousness of European humanism. An appreciation of rhetoric in the Americas, then, requires more than an occasional footnote in the standard histories of Renaissance rhetoric. My intent in the study that follows, therefore, is to provide the career of rhetoric in the New World with its own chapter in the long and complicated history of rhetoric.

Chapter 1

Rhetoric
Old World and New

In 1492 Antonio de Nebrija published the first grammar of a modern European language, *Gramática de la lengua castellana*. In his preface, addressed to Queen Isabella, Nebrija justifies his project in a way that his "very illustrious Queen" must surely have appreciated. One certain conclusion, proclaims Nebrija, is that "language has always been the companion of empire."[1] Nebrija could not have realized how truly prophetic this rationale for his little book was to be. The great Spanish humanist no doubt had in mind the role of Castilian in the rapid expansion of Castile and Aragon in the Iberian peninsula. His *Gramática* was published in the final year of the long war of the reconquest of Spain from the forces of Islam. Under the Catholic Monarchs Spain was becoming a major imperialist power, and Castilian was emerging as the national language. Yet in 1492 Nebrija could not have known just how immense the Spanish empire would soon become, nor could he know how linguistically varied the realms of the Catholic monarchs would ultimately be.

While Nebrija may not have fully anticipated the course of Spanish colonialism, he did appreciate the importance of language in human affairs. Nebrija shared the conviction of European humanists that human society was created and sustained by the gift of language. So passionate was this belief that Renaissance humanism itself has often been defined as the pursuit of eloquence.[2] That pursuit was in turn directed by a renewed attention to classical rhetorical theory.[3] The humanists' understanding of classical rhetoric was, to an extraordinary extent, shaped by one ancient authority, Marcus Tulius Cicero.[4]

Cicero, the greatest orator of republican Rome, argued that in the very beginning of human history an eloquent man, a great orator, created civil society by the power of persuasion. In his earliest rhetorical work, *De inventione*, Cicero describes the origin of "this thing we call eloquence" and recounts a time when "men wandered at large in the fields like animals and lived on wild fare; they did nothing by the guidance of reason, but relied chiefly on physical strength." Humans lived in this barbarous condition until "a man—great and wise I am sure—became aware of the power latent in man and the wide field offered by his mind for great achievements if one could develop this power and improve it by instruction." This great man assembled these brutes and, eventually, "through reason and eloquence . . . he transformed them from wild savages into a kind and gentle folk." This transformation, made possible by discourse "at the same time powerful and entrancing," marked the beginning of civilization.[5] Thus, civilized society derives from the uniquely human ability to use language and to use it well. Cicero says that men, "although lower and weaker than animals in many respects, excel them most by having the power of speech. Therefore that man appears to me to have won a splendid possession who excels men themselves in that ability by which men excel beasts."[6]

Cicero did not regard excellence in speech alone as sufficient to ensure the maintenance of civilization. Rather, he required that eloquence, rhetoric, be paired with wisdom, philosophy. In the famous passage with which *De inventione* begins Cicero declares that "wisdom without eloquence does too little for the good of the states, but that eloquence without wisdom is generally highly disadvantageous and is never helpful."[7] Convinced of an essentially reciprocal relationship of wisdom and eloquence, Cicero dedicated himself to accomplishing a union of the two ancient disciplines. His dedication to both rhetoric and philosophy inspired postclassical rhetoricians to continue to pursue this elusive union.

De inventione, together with the pseudo-Ciceronian *Ad Herennium*, became the principal sources of rhetorical theory in the Middle Ages.[8] The importance of *De inventione* to medieval writers ensured a continuing allegiance to Cicero's vision of rhetoric as a civilizing force. John Ward points out that from late medieval treatises there emerges, "rephrased, the essence of the myth of civilization with which *De inventione* opens and which was to so powerfully recommend that text to the attention of twelfth-century students."[9]

If students of the twelfth century were drawn to the mythic vision of *De inventione*'s introduction, later writers, especially those of the Quattrocentro and beyond, were truly preoccupied with the Ciceronian image of civilization's origins. Jerrold Seigel contends that, while there were many reasons for the humanists devotion to Cicero, one aspect of his work stood out:

Cicero was both a man of eloquence and a man of philosophy. He had an enormous respect for the great figures of Greek philosophy, and he found in their endeavors the answers to certain human needs which social life could not fully meet; thus he recommended the study of philosophy to his fellow citizens. But his own basic commitment was to the life of man in society, and his primary intellectual allegiance was to the culture of rhetoric. Balancing these two sets of loyalties, Cicero gave more attention than perhaps any other classical writer to the question of the relationship between rhetoric and philosophy.[10]

The Ciceronian conception of the orator, endowed with both eloquence and wisdom, as the agent of civilization became a widely accepted cultural ideal of Renaissance humanism. Little wonder, then, that the humanists invested such energy in the pursuit of eloquence. Thus, in Spain, as in all of Europe, rhetoric was a central intellectual and cultural concern. So great was this concern that George Saintsbury discovered in sixteenth-century Spain "a tolerably fair herd of humanist rhetoricians."[11] Saintsbury is correct—many of the greatest humanists of the Golden Age contributed to the development of Spanish rhetorical theory. Nebrija, for example, followed his *Gramática* with *Artis rhetoricae compendiosa* (1515). And Francisco Sánchez de las Brozas, Juan Luis Vives, Benito Arias Montano, Pedro Juan Nuñez, Luis de Granada, and many other Spanish humanists produced treatises on rhetoric.[12]

The continuity between these Renaissance rhetoricians and their ancient predecessors is conspicuous. Renaissance writers sought to distance themselves from what they perceived to be the limitations of medieval discourse by turning to classical models of eloquent expression. Indeed, much of Renaissance rhetoric is an effort to make the rhetorical precepts and principles of antiquity relevant to the markedly different circumstances of the sixteenth century. Renaissance rhetoricians in Spain and elsewhere, inspired by the Greeks and, especially, the Romans, sought to create a system of rhetoric which was faithful to its origins yet cognizant of a changing world.

This process of modification had been occurring since the origins of rhetoric as an intellectual system in fifth-century B.C.E. Athens. Rhetoric proved to be remarkably versatile in responding to changing cultural and political conditions. Neither the demise of Athenian democracy nor the rise and fall of Roman imperialism nor the triumph of Christianity over paganism had dislodged rhetoric from its central position in European intellectual life. In their own way Renaissance humanists were simply continuing the historical evolution of a venerable discipline.

This rather orderly evolution of rhetorical principles would be seriously challenged by the Columbian encounter and the subsequent course of Spanish colonialism. For the most part, Spanish rhetoricians, like their counterparts elsewhere in Europe, were preoccupied with reforming rhetoric for their immediate needs and gave little thought to how rhetoric might adapt to circumstances across the Atlantic. Few rhetoricians in Europe had any interest in crafting a rhetoric adapted to peoples unknown to Cicero—or, indeed, any Europeans until the fifteenth century. It is unlikely that rhetoricians ever faced a more difficult adaptation. To be sure, the Romans resisted early Greek efforts to teach rhetoric in Rome, and early Christians distrusted rhetoric because of its pagan associations. But these transitions, although difficult, were between people essentially alike. Greeks and Romans, pagans and Christians, coexisted in the Mediterranean world. Never had Europeans been confronted by humans so distant and so different. And never were rhetoricians required to consider how such different peoples might communicate with one another.

Critical questions, then, confronted rhetoricians as a result of the encounter: Could Europeans adapt their ancient art to the exigencies of a New World? Or would they ignore the customs and mores of the inhabitants of the Americas and perpetuate the centuries-old patterns of European thought? Or would these theorists find a "middle way" cognizant of both the classical heritage and the indigenous experience? The complex and varied responses to these questions, offered by rhetoricians in Spain and across the "ocean sea," are the subject of this study.

The Two Rhetorics of Luis de Granada

The problems and potentialities presented by the encounter to Renaissance rhetoric become apparent in the works of Luis de Granada (1504–88). Granada looked back to the rhetoric of antiquity, while he also looked across the seas to envision an evangelical rhetoric suited to the "newly discovered" lands. Granada was one of the very few Europeans to do both. While the Renaissance produced numerous rhetorical treatises and European expansion required many missionary manuals, Granada was very nearly alone in considering the rhetorical requirements of European Christians and indigenous Americans. Thus, Granada's writings are a useful index of how the art of rhetoric might adapt to the needs of the two worlds of the sixteenth century.

Granada, one of the great preachers of Renaissance Europe, was delighted to learn that there were people in the "new worlds that in our days have been discovered" who desired to learn of the Christian faith. To accommodate these curious heathens Granada wrote the *Breve tratado en que se declara de la manera que se podrá proponer la doctrina de nuestra santa fe y religión cristiana á los nuevos fieles* (*A Brief Treatise which Declares the Manner by which the Doctrine of our Holy Faith and Christian Religion can be Propounded to New Believers*).[13] This little work was intended to guide missionaries in their efforts to propagate Christianity among the peoples of the East and West Indies. As such, the *Breve tratado* represents an early European effort to consider how the unfamiliar inhabitants of exotic lands might be persuaded to accept the Christian faith.

Granada wrote another, and very different, book about Christian preaching entitled the *Ecclesiasticae rhetoricae* (1576).[14] This ecclesiastical rhetoric was designed to aid the orator as he preached not to the inhabitants of strange new worlds but, instead, to the familiar audiences of the Old World. These European audiences, Granada assumed, had long since been converted to Christianity, so in the *Ecclesiaticae rhetoricae* he addressed not conversion but, rather, persuasion designed to intensify Christian's faith and, most important, to act in accordance with it. Thus, while both the *Breve tratado* and the *Ecclesiaticae rhetoricae* were intended for the Christian orator, the two works are, in many respects, fundamentally different endeavors. Both, however, represent efforts by Granada to adapt ancient traditions to the new circumstances of the sixteenth century caused by Europe's geographic expansion and religious fragmentation.

Granada's *Ecclesiasticae rhetoricae* is an important example of how a classically oriented rhetoric might respond to the complexities of Renaissance Europe. After all, the *Ecclesiaticae rhetoricae* was derived from a rhetorical tradition that was already virtually a thousand years old in the sixteenth century. Granada, however, was not content simply to transmit tradition but was intent on adapting his ancient subject to the particular demands of the Renaissance.

The *Ecclesiasticae rhetoricae* was in part a response to the call of the Council of Trent (1545–63) to revitalize Catholicism in the face of the Protestant challenge. In particular, Granada was prompted by the

Council's desire to rehabilitate the practice of Catholic preaching. As Anne J. Cruz and Mary Elizabeth Perry indicate, "the Council of Trent institutionalized preaching as a means of rhetorically controlling the people and of disseminating social propaganda that encouraged the status quo. In its attempt to regularize oratory, the Church formulated a religious discourse intended to instruct, entertain, and persuade."[15] In other words, the Church mandated preaching based on the duties of the Ciceronian orator. Gwendolyn Barnes-Karol summarizes the extent of the problem addressed by the council:

> Although preaching had traditionally been a part of the propagation of Christianity, by as early as the fifth century it had already begun to be overshadowed by the liturgy of the mass. . . . In spite of the proliferation of medieval *artes praedicandi* and preachers' aids, preaching soon became an activity of particular religious orders (especially the Franciscans and Dominicans) rather than an essential duty of all secular and religious clergy. By the mid-1500s, Spain was plagued by a dearth of preachers despite the fact that there was no shortage of priests or members of religious orders. That situation was to change as Tridentine mandates concerning the regulation and standardization of clerical duties required that priests, for the first time ever, preach sermons every Sunday and feast days as well as daily during Advent and Lent. Thus began a period (which would last throughout the entire seventeenth century) of mobilizing and training the Spanish clergy to be transmitters of the Church's discourse of religious, moral, and socioeconomic orthodoxy.[16]

Granada makes it clear at the outset of the *Ecclesiasticae rhetoricae* that the decline of effective preaching resulted from neglecting rhetoric in the preacher's education. Why, he asks, when the other arts necessary to sacred theology are well studied, "do we not undertake equally the art of speaking well, so that we can exercise it felicitously in the employ of the preacher?"[17] The "other arts" of philosophy, theology, and dialectic are indeed necessary to the preacher's development, but they cannot substitute for the study of rhetoric. Granada believed that wisdom, theology, had been emphasized to the neglect of eloquence, rhetoric. Thus, the early chapters of the *Ecclesiasticae rhetoricae* are dominated by Granada's efforts to reassert the Ciceronian ideal of the union of wisdom and eloquence by achieving a proper place for rhetoric in the education of the preacher. While early church leaders had accommodated pagan rhetoric to Christianity, Granada believed that accommodation was not yet complete. Certainly, the medieval preaching manuals, the *artes praedicandi,* were not complete rhetorics in the Ciceronian tradition. Thus, while Granada's *Ecclesiasticae rhetoricae* is clearly Ciceronian, it is Ciceronianism in service to the Christian orator.[18]

At first glance the *Ecclesiasticae rhetoricae* appears to be more devoted to maintaining the rhetorical tradition than to adapting that tradition to the circumstances of the sixteenth century. The work is divided into five books. Book 1 discusses the general nature of rhetoric and the requirements of the preacher. Book 2 defines rhetoric and examines rhetorical invention. Book 3 expounds on amplification and the emotions. Book 4 considers the categories of sermons and disposition. Book 5, the longest of the books, details elocution. Finally, book 6 discusses delivery and returns to book 1's theme of the preacher's character. While this structure is certainly Ciceronian, Granada is not reluctant to alter that tradition when the needs of the Christian orator require that he do so. Thus, he omits a consideration of judicial oratory, one of the three standard genres of discourse, because it is irrelevant to preaching. Granada retains the two remaining genres of oratory, deliberative and epideictic, while altering their functions. Deliberative, or political, oratory is now devoted to the correction of the faults of sinners. In a similar fashion epideictic, the oratory of praise and blame, is directed toward praising the saints. Granada omits memory, one of the five traditional parts of rhetoric, because memory is a part of nature. While Granada alters or omits important elements of the Ciceronian tradition, he expands other aspects of Roman theory.

This is particularly apparent in Granada's treatment of amplification. *Amplificatio,* the process of expanding and intensifying discourse, had long been a standard part of rhetorical theory. Granada, however, goes beyond most traditional treatments and devotes an entire book to amplification. Although he does not do so explicitly, Granada very nearly elevates amplification to one of the fundamental parts of rhetoric. *Amplificatio* assumes great importance in the *Ecclesiasticae rhetoricae* because it is the means by which the orator engages the emotions that are critical to the preacher's success.

Granada apparently assumes that the preacher's audience will be composed of at least nominal Christians. Therefore, the task is not to get them to believe Christian dogma as much as it is to get them to act in accordance with that dogma. The only sure way to move an audience to action is through an emotional commitment, which can best be achieved by *amplificatio.* Amplification is, for Granada, as it was for the ancients, both a stylistic and an argumentative process.[19] As such, it incorporates aspects of both *elocutio* and *inventio.* Indeed, it seems as if Granada combed classical texts for the scattered references to amplification and incorporated them into a coherent treatment. The treatment of amplification makes clear that, while there is a place for argument in the Christian orator's arsenal, emotion is very often the more potent weapon.

Granada advocates appealing to the emotions of the audience, provided, of course, that such appeals are directed toward a noble end and are made by a responsible rhetor. Consequently, Granada devotes a good deal of attention to the character of the speaker. Indeed, the *Ecclesiasticae rhetoricae* virtually begins and ends with advice for the formulation of the preacher's persona. Granada conceives of this concern with character not so much as the ethos of classical rhetoric, a type of proof to be manipulated in the speech, but simply as an essential aspect of the preacher's life.

Granada's *Ecclesiasticae rhetoricae* is a long and thorough work that in broad outline, at least, follows the Ciceronian pattern. Granada did not simply replicate classical approaches but altered them when he believed it necessary. Despite the accommodation of Christian theology and pagan learning accomplished by the early Middle Ages, rhetorics that truly integrated the two remained remarkably rare. Granada, responding to the Protestant apostasy and Tridentine reformism, created one of the first such treatises.

The *Ecclesiasticae rhetoricae,* a detailed, mature statement of Christian Ciceronianism, presents a considerable contrast with the other Granadine rhetoric, the *Breve tratado.* As the name indicates, the *Breve tratado* is a concise account of how one might preach to peoples neither European nor Christian. Granada says he was prompted to write this book "because in the East Indies there are some kings who wish to embrace our sacred faith and religion, it occurred to me to propose some method by which they might conveniently accomplish this."[20] The *Breve tratado* is not only directed toward "East Indian kings," but is also a response to Granada's concern about the challenges to Catholicism. In this work the threat of the Protestant Reformation is even more apparent than it is in the *Ecclesiasticae rhetoricae.* Granada says that Germany and England, where once flowed "the fountains of the waters of grace and wisdom, were made sterile and fruitless by their heresies."[21] While in Europe the domain of the true faith was thus constricted, elsewhere the opposite occurred, and the faith expanded in "the lands of the Orient and the Occident, and in the new worlds that in our days have been discovered."[22]

Granada assumes, at the outset of the *Breve tratado*, that the peoples of the Indies are rational: "Before their conversion the heathens give no assent to the Sacred Scriptures, but rely on reason (which is a natural light which God instilled in our understanding, and which no man lacks)."[23] This fundamental assumption of indigenous rationality determines the strategy that Granada adopts in the *Breve tratado*. The possibility of a universal human rationality would also be a matter of intense controversy in Spain and a matter of great importance in directing Spanish colonial policy.[24] Although not one of the main protagonists in this debate, Granada in the *Breve tratado* is clearly an advocate of the fundamental reasonableness of all human beings.

A corollary to universal rationality is a common human desire "to know God and to know how to serve and honor Him."[25] Given an innate rationality and an instinctive curiosity about God, Granada recommends a straightforward approach to proselytizing. What is required is a presentation of Christian doctrine "in a few words."[26] The *Breve tratado* is just such a summary, representing a distillation of Granada's longest work, *Introducción al símbolo de la fe* (1582–85). Granada recommends beginning with the simplest tenets of Christianity and gradually progressing to more complex beliefs. He therefore begins the *Breve tratado* with a discussion of the existence of God and the impossibility of the existence of other gods. Only after these premises are established can the missionary progress to the more elusive concepts of the Holy Trinity, the incarnation of Christ, and the seven sacraments. In the *Breve tratado* Granada is content to present only the most fundamental of Christian beliefs and makes no attempt to offer a complete theological exposition.

Because the first step in the missionary process is belief, rather than action, the emotional approach emphasized in the *Ecclesiasticae rhetoricae* is absent. Missing, in fact, are virtually all the rhetorical apparatus so important in the *Ecclesiasticae rhetoricae*. There is no discussion of invention nor style nor delivery nor amplification. A simple, rational approach will suffice for the new believer, whereas the Christians of Europe require all of the techniques developed over the ages.

The contrasts between the *Breve tratado* and the *Ecclesiasticae rhetoricae* illuminate the difficulties facing Granada, or any European, who might attempt to write a rhetoric in response to the encounter. Granada had great interest in the enterprise of the Indies and had plans, never fulfilled, to travel to the New World.[27] He was, therefore, without direct experience of the peoples of the Americas. Yet Granada did have a lifetime of experience preaching to the Christians of Spain and Portugal. It is perhaps not surprising, therefore, that the *Ecclesiasticae rhetoricae* is far more detailed than the *Breve tratado*. In writing the *Ecclesiasticae rhetoricae*, Granada could draw on his career as a Christian orator as well as centuries of rhetorical tradition. More than Granada's own career, these ancient traditions, revitalized by the Renaissance, made the adaptation of rhetoric to the needs of the New World especially elusive. The strength of the classical rhetorical tradition combined with the political ambitions and religious intolerance of late medieval and Renaissance Spain served to inhibit the fashioning of an entirely new rhetoric to accompany Europe's encounters with the peoples of the New World.

Persuasion, Conversion, and Coercion

The early Christian church distrusted rhetoric and, indeed, all things pagan. Rhetoric was eventually accepted by Christianity as a result of the sympathetic treatment by early church leaders, including Aurelius Augustine in *De doctrina christiana* (completed 426–27). That the early accommodation between Christianity and rhetoric did not erase all the tensions between the two is apparent in Granada's *Ecclesiasticae rhetoricae*. Even in the sixteenth century Granada felt it necessary to attempt a more thorough integration of Ciceronianism and Christianity than may have existed even after more than a millennium of Christian ascendancy in Europe. The integration Granada desired was inhibited by a fundamental disagreement about the nature of the persuasive process. Whereas classical rhetoric is predicated upon probable reasoning and human decision making, Christianity, in contrast, assumes divine revelation and spiritual intervention in mortal matters. These differences are sometimes seen in the distinctions, both theological and rhetorical, between persuasion and conversion. Augustine's *De doctrina christiana*, which did much to legitimize rhetoric to Christians is, in book 4, a treatise on religious persuasion, not conversion. As George Kennedy explains:

Augustine, like earlier Christians, regarded conversion as an act of the spirit in which eloquence has no true role. The work is addressed to Christian teachers, chiefly the clergy, and explains how to discover Christian knowledge and how to expand it to a converted, but ignorant or lethargic audience. The function of Christian eloquence in Augustine's system is to convert belief into works, to impel the faithful to the Christian life. This had become an important consideration and remained one permanently now that Christianity was the established religion of the state and that the Church numbered many nominal members who lacked the intensity and dedication characteristic of earlier Christians.[28]

In Augustine's estimation, then, rhetoric serves to impel the converted to act consistently with their beliefs.

Conversion, on the other hand, is discussed by Augustine in *De catechizandis rudibus* (397). *De catechizandis* is addressed to Deogratias, a Carthaginian bishop, who had sought advice from Augustine on how to instruct the unconverted. This advice is given in two parts: a discussion of conversion methods and an extended example illustrating how conversion might be accomplished. Augustine recommends instruction that consists of a narration of Old Testament history and the coming of Christ followed by an exhortation revealing the resurrection of Christ and the promise of the salvation of humankind. Although Augustine's model address is rather brief, he explains that, if it taxes the patience of the converts, the address can be abbreviated, but it should not be lengthened.[29]

The early Christian's suspicion of rhetoric is apparent in *De catechizandis*. Augustine warns that a cleric may encounter students from the schools of rhetoric who wish instruction. Such men can be included neither "among the illiterate, nor yet among those very learned men whose minds have been trained by the investigation of serious questions." These rhetoricians must come to understand that, "though sometimes the language of the law courts may be called good speaking, it can never be called holy speaking."[30] Despite these and other uncomplimentary remarks, Augustine displays considerable ambivalence toward rhetoric. As Thomas Conley notes, most of what Augustine says "about audience adaptation and the problems of 'instructing' the 'uncultivated' reads as though he had the *De oratore* of Cicero, if not at his elbow, at least at the back of his mind."[31] Indeed, if conversion were exclusively an act of faith, there would seem to be little need for the rather detailed discussions of audience adaptation which appear in *De catechizandis.*

While the distinction between persuasion and conversion, rhetoric and faith, is not always precise in Augustine, the contrast between a complex rhetorical theory aimed at the converted and a simpler theological exposition directed at the uninitiated is clearly established in *De doctrina* and *De catechizandis.* This dichotomy is largely replicated in Granada's *Ecclesiasticae rhetoricae* and his *Breve tratado.* Granada's perpetuation of the Augustinian distinction between persuasion and conversion would have serious implications for the development of rhetoric in the New World. The variations between the *Ecclesiasticae rhetoricae* and the *Breve tratado* strongly suggested that rhetoric would be reserved for Europeans, while only a simpler catechistic approach would be appropriate for the Amerindians. Granada, then, establishes a precedent for a dichotomous conception of the audience in the sixteenth century.

The Columbian encounter clearly complicated the role of audience in rhetorical theory. From the very inception of rhetoric theorists had recognized that persuasion required understanding human nature and appealing to its various dimensions. Granada himself clearly perceives the importance of audience—as his extensive treatment of *amplificatio* and the emotions in the *Ecclesiasticae rhetoricae* demonstrates. He also recognizes possible variations between audiences and the importance of adapting to these differences. Yet Granada's appreciation of the potential variations among listeners is quite limited. Listeners may well be less educated and less sophisticated than the speaker, but these are differences of degree rather than of kind. For the most part Granada, like theorists before him, conceives of an audience as an assemblage of people linked to the speaker by nationality and language. Even in the *Breve tratado* Granada shows little concern with the possibility of encountering an audience truly alien to the speaker.

Preachers of the Golden Age clearly recognized the importance of adapting to the variations of Spanish audiences.[32] These preachers were particularly adept at appealing to popular audiences with carefully orchestrated performances and ingenious histrionics. Granada, as a skilled preacher and stylist, certainly knew the value of such an approach. Here too, however, the audiences differed in degree but not in kind. Thus, in both theory and practice sixteenth-century Spaniards recognized the necessity of adapting to various audiences—but within recognized, familiar limits. Nothing in the rhetorical tradition could ready even a preacher as accomplished as Granada to conceive of an audience composed of the "other."[33]

It was not only uncertainty about the nature of the audience, however, which made the construction of a rhetoric aimed at the New World experience difficult. The course of Spanish history immediately prior to and contemporaneous with the encounter would prove to be inhospitable to the development of a missionary rhetoric. As Spain expanded geographically and coalesced politically, a "culture of control" developed in the imperial domains.[34] Spanish imperialism and the Protestant expansion encouraged a degree of conformity previously regarded as unnecessary. Jews and Muslims, long tolerated in Spain, were now required to convert to Christianity and integrate into Spanish culture. The perceived need to convert large numbers of nonbelievers would seem to present a perfect situation for the engagement of the highly developed theorist of preaching. Such, unfortunately, was not the case. The fateful year 1492 witnessed a massive effort to achieve a conversion by coercive, rather than rhetorical, methods.

The most dramatic example of coercive conversion, but far from the only example, occurred in 1492 when the crown ordered the expulsion from Castile and Aragon of all Jews who refused to convert to Christianity. As a result, some 100,000 Jews were expelled, while about 50,000 chose to remain in Spain and accept Christianity. While the reasons for the expulsion are complex, the conversion of the Jews was an important factor. Henry Kamen claims that "there can be absolutely no doubt that *the decree had conversion, not expulsion, as its motive.* . . . On this point both King and Inquisition appear to have coincided. . . . Indeed it is possible to maintain that during these years, in *every* case for which we have evidence, and above all for Spain, the motive of legislation was not expulsion, but contemporary conversion."[35]

The conversion of the Islamic population was attempted in much the same way. In 1492 the emirate of Granada was defeated by the Catholic Monarchs, and the long *reconquista* was finally over. With the reconquest a large number of Muslims were added to the Spanish population, thus intensifying the perceived need to achieve widespread Christianization. Early attempts at the peaceful persuasion of the "Moors" had not met with rapid success. Thus, more extreme measures seemed warranted. The crown sent Francisco Jiménez de Cisneros, archbishop of Toledo, to Andalusia to supervise the conversion campaign. Cisneros promptly initiated a program of mass conversions of Muslims, which provoked a revolt. The revolt was repressed in 1501, and, in the same year, all Muslims in Granada were ordered to convert to Christianity. In 1502 a decree was issued which required all Muslims in Castile to be baptized or be expelled.[36] As with the Jews before them, thousand of Muslims fled Spain, and thousands more chose to remain as new converts to the only acceptable religion in the peninsula.

Such an approach to the conversion of a sizable population professing aberrant beliefs had certain obvious advantages: conversion could be implemented almost immediately by administrative fiat, thereby obviating the need for a long and difficult persuasive campaign. Despite the apparent efficiency of such an approach to Christianization, conversion by decree resulted in some obvious disadvantages. Because the conversion had been extorted, neither the sincerity of the converts nor the longevity of the conversion could ever be entirely trusted. Christianized Jewish *converso* families, in particular, were mistrusted for generations. Moreover, the threat of backsliding required constant monitoring of the convert's fidelity. This monitoring became institutionalized with the advent of the Inquisition. *Moriscos, conversos,* Lutherans, Erasmians, and other threats to orthodoxy required constant vigilance. Thus, while conversion by decree was initially efficient, it was a policy that necessitated recurrent coercion.

Not only did the program of forced conversion require an institutionalized apparatus of control, it probably also deterred the development of a true missionary rhetoric. The reliance on coercion meant there was little incentive to develop an evangelical rhetoric for use in the Iberian peninsula. The absence of practical experience and theoretical investigation of peaceful persuasion in Spain meant that there was remarkably little information about religious conversion which could be readily transferred to Spain's colonies. Granada's two works reflect both the dominance of traditional rhetoric and the relatively inchoate state of missionary rhetoric in Spain.

The prospects for developing a rhetorical theory that might adapt to the needs of the New World were far from propitious. Neither the rhetorical traditions of Rome nor the conversion practices of fifteenth- and sixteenth-century Spain did much to prepare rhetoricians of the time for the challenges created by the encounter. On the other hand, the difficulties were not so great as to be insurmountable. Renaissance Spain had inherited centuries of accumulated advice and experience about the means of persuading human beings. Moreover, rhetoric had itself demonstrated remarkable adaptability in new cultural encounters—from Greek to Roman, from pagan to Christian. It would seem possible, at least, that rhetoricians might be able to accomplish one more adaptation of their art—from European to American. What would be required, in large measure, were theorists who had been exposed to the New World and its peoples. For rhetoric to meet this newest challenge required rhetors who would live and write among the natives of the New World. Men doing just that were already at work in the Americas as Granada was writing his *Ecclesiasticae rhetoricae.* Just as Granada created a fusion of Ciceronian and pagan rhetoric, others would attempt a fusion of the rhetoric of the Old World and the discourse of the New.

Notes

1. *Gramática de la lengua castellana,* ed. Antonio Quilis (Madrid: Editora Nacional, 1980), 97.

2. Hanna Gray, "Renaissance Humanism: The Pursuit of Eloquence," in *Renaissance Essays from the Journal of the History of Ideas,* ed. Paul O. Kristeller and Philip P. Weiner (New York: Harper, 1968), 199–216; Jerrold E. Seigel, *Rhetoric and Philosophy in Renaissance Humanism: The Union of Eloquence and Wisdom, Petrarch to Valla* (Princeton: Princeton University Press, 1968); Nancy S. Struever, *The Language of History in the Renaissance: Rhetoric and Historical Consciousness in Florentine Humanism* (Princeton: Princeton University Press, 1970).

3. The literature on Renaissance rhetoric is vast. Particularly useful introductions include: John Monfasani, "Rhetoric and Humanism," in *Renaissance Humanism: Foundation, Forms, and Legacy,* vol. 3: *Humanism and the Disciplines,* ed. Albert Rabil Jr. (Philadelphia: University of Pennsylvania Press, 1988), 171–235; James J. Murphy, ed., *Renaissance Eloquence; Studies in the Theory and Practice of Renaissance Rhetoric* (Berkeley: University of California Press, 1983); Brian Vickers, "Renaissance Reintegration," in *In Defense of Rhetoric* (Oxford: Oxford University Press, 1990); Don Paul Abbott, "The Renaissance," in *The Present State of Scholarship in Historical and Contemporary Rhetoric,* ed. Winifred Bryan Horner, rev. ed. (Columbia: University of Missouri Press, 1990), 84–113.

4. For the influence of Cicero in the Renaissance, see the works listed in nn. 2 and 3. See also Izora Scott, *Controversies over the Imitation of Cicero as a Model for Style and Some Phases of Their Influence on the Schools of the Renaissance* (New York: Teachers College, Columbia University, 1910); and John O. Ward, "Renaissance Commentators on Ciceronian Rhetoric," in *Renaissance Eloquence,* 126–73. For Cicero's influence in Spain, see Rebecca Switzer, *The Ciceronian Style in Fr. Luis de Granada* (New York: Instituto de España, 1927), esp. chap. 1, "Fr. Luis De Granada and Ciceronianism in Spain," 1–35.

5. *De inventione,* trans. H. M. Hubbell, Loeb Classical Library (Cambridge: Harvard University Press, 1968), I.i–ii. Cicero in turn had borrowed this version from the Greek Isocrates. In the *Antidosis* Isocrates says, "because there has been implanted in us the power to persuade each other and to make clear to each other whatever we desire, not only have we escaped the life of wild beasts, but we have come together and founded cities and made laws and invented arts; and, generally speaking, there is no institution devised by man which the power of speech has not helped us establish" (trans. G. B. Norlin, Loeb Classical Library [Cambridge: Harvard University Press, 1962], 254–56).

6. Ibid., I.iv.5.

7. Ibid., I.i.1.

8. For a comprehensive account of the attention devoted to both *De inventione* and the *Ad Herennium* by medieval scholars, see John O. Ward, "From Antiquity to the Renaissance: Glosses and Commentaries on Cicero's *Rhetorica,* in *Medieval Eloquence: Studies in the Theory and Practice of Medieval Rhetoric,* ed. James J. Murphy (Berkeley: University of California Press, 1978), 25–67.

9. Ibid., 46.

10. Siegel, *Rhetoric and Philosophy,* 5.

11. *A History of Criticism and Literary Taste in Europe* (Edinburgh: Blackwood, 1902), 235–36.

12. For comprehensive accounts of Spanish Renaissance rhetoric, see Antonio Martí, *La preceptiva retórica en el Siglo de Oro* (Madrid: Editorial Gredos, 1972); José Rico Verdú, *La retórica española de los siglos XVI y XVII* (Madrid: Consejo Superior de Investigaciones Científicas, 1973); Elena Artaza, *El ars narrandi en el siglo XVI español. Teoría y práctica* (Duesto: University of Duesto, 1989); and Luisa López Grigera, "An Introduction to the Study of Rhetoric in 16th Century Spain," *Dispositio* 8 (1983): 1–64.

13. This work was originally intended to be the fifth part of Granada's *Símbolo de la fe* (1583). See *Obras de Fray Luis de Granada,* vol. 2: *Biblioteca de autores españoles* (Madrid: Atlas, 1945), 596. The *Breve tratado* was first published separately in 1585. Maximino Llaneza's bibliography of Granada's works lists at least sixteen subsequent editions or printings of this work, including French and Italian translations (*Bibliografía del V. P. M. Fr. Luis de Granada* [Salamanca: Calatrava, 1926], 4:294). The Italian translation, item 758, does not appear in Llaneza's index. See 1:287.

14. Llaneza's *Bibliografía* list some forty-five editions of this work in Latin, Spanish, and French. This number excludes those versions included in various editions of Granada's collected works. I am using the Spanish translation commissioned by Bishop Climent in the eighteenth century and included in *Obras, Biblioteca de autores españoles,* 3:493–642.

15. "Introduction," *Culture and Control in Counter-Reformation Spain* (Minneapolis: University of Minnesota Press, 1992), xv–xvi.

16. "Religious Oratory in a Culture of Control," in Cruz and Perry, *Culture and Control,* 53.

17. *Obras*, 3:494.

18. For a comprehensive survey of medieval theories of preaching, see James J. Murphy, *Rhetoric in the Middle Ages: A History of Rhetorical Theory from St. Augustine to the Renaissance* (Berkeley: University of California Press, 1974), 269–363. Granada was not, of course, the only Renaissance rhetorician who sought to rehabilitate Christian rhetoric. For a thorough treatment of this problem, see Debra Shuger, *Sacred Rhetoric: The Christian Grand Style in the English Renaissance* (Princeton: Princeton University Press, 1988), 55–117. For a discussion of Tridentine rhetorics in particular, see 76–80. See also Marc Fumaroli, *L'Age de l'éloquence: Rhétorique et "res literaria" de la Renaissance au seuil de l'époque classique* (Paris: Albin Michel, 1994), 116–61. For Granada see 143–48.

19. For a discussion of the Ciceronian antecedents of Granada's treatment of amplification see Switzer, *Ciceronian Style*, chaps. 3 and 4.

20. *Obras*, 2:598.

21. Ibid., 2:596.

22. Ibid.

23. Ibid., 2:598.

24. Granada may have been influenced in this matter by another Dominican, Bartolomé de las Casas, the leading proponent of the rationality and intelligence of the New World's peoples. See Bartolomé de las Casas, *In Defense of the Indians*, ed. and trans. Stafford Poole, C.M. (DeKalb: Northern Illinois University Press, 1992).

25. *Obras*, 2:598.

26. Ibid.

27. For a discussion of Granada's attempt to visit the Indies, see Alvaro Huerga, *Fray Luis de Granada: Una vida al servicio de la Iglesia* (Madrid: Biblioteca de Autores Cristianos, 1988), 34–46.

28. *Classical Rhetoric and Its Christian and Secular Tradition from Ancient to Modern Times* (Chapel Hill: University of North Carolina Press, 1980), 157–58.

29. *The First Catechetical Instruction [De Catechizandis Rudibus]*, trans. Joseph P. Christopher (Westminster, Md.: Newman Press, 1962), 51–81, 83.

30. Ibid., 33–34.

31. *Rhetoric in the European Tradition* (New York: Longman, 1990), 75.

32. For discussions of Spanish preaching during this time, see, in addition to Barnes-Karol, "Religious Oratory in a Culture of Control," in Cruz and Perry, *Culture and Control*, 51–77; and Hilary Dansey Smith, *Preaching in the Spanish Golden Age: A Study of Some Preachers of the Reign of Philip III* (Oxford: Oxford University Press, 1978).

33. For a particularly detailed discussion of the concept of the "other," see Tzvetan Todorov, *The Conquest of America: The Question of the Other*, trans. Richard Howard (New York: Harper, 1984).

34. See Cruz and Perry, "Introduction," *Culture and Control*, ix–xxiii.

35. "The Expulsion: Purpose and Consequence," in *Spain and the Jews: The Sephardi Experience 1492 and After,* ed. Elie Kedourie (London: Thames and Hudson, 1992), 81.

36. For accounts of the conversion of the Islamic population of Spain, see Anwar G. Chejne, *Islam and the West: The Moriscos* (Albany: State University of New York Press, 1983), 1–16; and L. P. Harvey, *Islamic Spain: 1250 to 1500* (Chicago: University of Chicago Press, 1990), esp. 129–31.

Chapter 2

Bernardino de Sahagún and the Rhetoric of the Other

Bernardino de Sahagún arrived in New Spain in 1529, just eight years after the fall of the Aztec capital of Tenochtitlán. This Franciscan friar's arrival in the New World came only four years after the first twelve missionaries of his order had begun the "spiritual conquest" of Mexico. Like the "twelve apostles" before him, Sahagún was sent to Mexico as an agent of the great Franciscan evangelistic enterprise in the New World.[1] Sahagún proved to be not only an evangelist but a most accomplished ethnographer as well. He was a serious and sensitive observer of the life of the Mexica people and, more importantly, a thorough and indefatigable recorder of what he observed. Indeed, historians are deeply indebted to Sahagún as an essential source of knowledge about Mexica life prior to and immediately after the conquest. So extraordinary was Sahagún's work, claims Jorge Klor de Alva, that it "led to the first examples of modern ethnographic fieldwork and narrative, thereby genuinely making him the first modern anthropologist."[2]

Just as Sahagún virtually pioneered ethnography, so too did he anticipate what would eventually be called intercultural communication. Sahagún was one of the first Europeans to hear and to preserve the public speeches of the "other." Thus, an understanding of the role of rhetoric in an Amerindian culture must begin with Sahagún. Relatively few other Europeans, of course, had the opportunity to hear the speeches of the Mexica so soon after the conquest. But, more importantly, even fewer recognized the necessity of preserving the discourse of the natives.

Sahagún and others, by diligently recording the orations of the Mexica, provided posterity with a remarkable record of the rhetoric of a predominantly oral society. Historians of Mexico have long recognized that an examination of these speeches provides insights into the thought and culture of the Mexica which is unavailable from any other source. To the historian of rhetoric the orations preserved by Sahagún are equally invaluable because they constitute one of the most complete accounts of the rhetoric of an ancient, non-European culture. Thus, an examination of Mexica oratory is instructive of the role of rhetoric in the life of the early Mexicans and may be indicative of the function of rhetoric in non-European societies generally. Moreover, the discourse of these Mesoamericans offers additional evidence with which to reconstruct the elusive origins of rhetoric in human consciousness.

The Ancient Word

The early Franciscan friars were remarkably sensitive to the cultural and linguistic accomplishments of the natives of the New World. The friars recognized that among the Mexica were men of exceptional oratorical abilities. What the Franciscans knew as rhetoric, the Mexica themselves called *huehuehtlahtolli,* a Nahuatl word formed by compounding *huehue,* "old man" or "men of old," and *tlahtolli,* "word", "oration," or "language." Thus, *huehuehtlahtolli* is variously translated as the "ancient word," the "speeches of the ancients," or the "speeches of the elders." According to Thelma Sullivan, the term may well have both meanings. That is, *huehuehtlahtolli* signifies the speeches of the ancients, orations originally given by the ancestors of the sixteenth-century Mexica, as well as the speeches of the elders, addresses presented by men of advanced age and high status.[3]

These *huehuehtlahtolli* are preserved in many of the chronicles of sixteenth- and seventeenth-century Mexico. The most important collection of these speeches and probably the most significant source of information about the preconquest Mexica is found in the work of the indefatigable Friar Sahagún. Sahagún was born in Spain, probably in 1499. He studied at Salamanca and was, like many of the Franciscan missionaries to Mexico, well educated in humanistic tradition. He lived in New Spain from his arrival in 1529 until his death in 1590.[4] Sahagún was an accomplished linguist who mastered Nahuatl, the language of the Mexica and the lingua franca of Central Mexico. Consistent with Franciscan policy in the New World, Sahagún employed Nahuatl in his efforts to educate and convert the Mexica. He wrote extensively on his experiences in Mexico, producing numerous works in Spanish, Latin, and Nahuatl on theological, philological, historical, and anthropological subjects. Many of these treatises exist only in manuscripts or fragments, and some, like his Spanish-Nahuatl dictionary and grammar, are lost.[5]

Sahagún's masterpiece is *The General History of New Spain*.[6] This work is composed of twelve books, which detail the history, beliefs, customs, and daily activities of the Mexica. The *General History* was the result of an unprecedented ethnographic enterprise. Sahagún assembled a group of Indian informants, "prominent old men," chosen for their knowledge of Mexica customs, together with some younger Indian "grammarians," who assisted with the necessary recording and translation. Sahagún probed his informants for their knowledge of the traditions and practices of Mexica life before the conquest. By 1547 he had elicited from his informants the *huehuehtlahtolli* that figure so prominently in the *General History*. These "old men" of 1547 who recited the *huehuehtlahtolli* and provided so much other information would have been middle-aged at the time of the conquest and hence fully versed in life before the arrival of the Spanish. Despite his reliance on knowledgeable native sources and the systematic nature of his inquiries, Sahagún's methods remain problematic. Inga Clendinnen says that "with all its defects—produced by survivors of the erstwhile ruling group; exclusively male; further distanced from the actuality we seek to glimpse by its idealizing tendency and its Spanish eliciting and editing; abducted into English," the *General History* "is nonetheless the best source we have for Mexica views, and for accounts of Mexica action as described by Mexica voices."[7] Thus, the *General History* remains, for Clendinnen, and anyone else who seeks to understand the Mexica, "that indispensable text."[8]

Sahagún's "indispensable text" was researched, written, revised, and edited over a period of nearly fifty years. A Nahuatl text was completed in 1569; a bilingual Spanish-Nahuatl version was produced in 1577. Unfortunately, Sahagún did not live to see his manuscript published. Possibly because of royal opposition or perhaps simply due to bureaucratic indifference, the work, although complete, never reached the printing press. This unfortunate neglect continued for centuries. The *General History* was finally published in 1929–30. Of the three manuscripts of the *General History* prepared by Sahagún the most complete is the *Florentine Codex*, so called because it is located in the Laurentian Library, Florence. The manuscript is written in Nahuatl and Spanish, arranged in parallel columns. Arthur J. O. Anderson and Charles Dibble, the translators of the English version used here, chose to render the Nahuatl into English so that "the structures of the translations would resemble as closely as possible that of the original. Since the Spanish text of the *Florentine Codex* was Sahagún's sixteenth-century Spanish, the English translation of the Nahuatl was to parallel, in a sense, the late Renais-

sance feeling of Sahagún's Spanish through the employment of occasional archaisms which might give it something of the atmosphere of
the King James version of the Bible. This procedure, while it precludes a
translation which would be word for word a precise duplicate (in English), would, it was felt, still preserve sufficient accuracy in its presentation of the meaning of the Aztec version."[9]

The *huehuehtlahtolli* that Sahagún collected in 1547 ultimately became book 6 of the *General History,* entitled "Of the Rhetoric and Moral
Philosophy of the Mexican People." Sahagún made a conscientious attempt to reproduce faithfully, in Nahuatl, the orations recited by his
Mexica interlocutors. The *huehuehtlahtolli* presented in book 6, in particular, reflect the uncertainties inherent in Sahagún's undertaking. The
speeches were elicited by Sahagún, recited orally by his informants, transcribed by assistants of uncertain linguistic and literary ability, and eventually translated into Spanish. Thus, the *huehuehtlahtolli* are subject to all
the difficulties of translating both from the spoken to the written word
and from Nahuatl to the Spanish.[10] Given these challenges, Sahagún
seems to have been remarkably successful in his efforts. According to
Francis Kartunnen and James Lockhart, "it now begins to appear that
Spanish translators of the generation of Sahagún, once thought to have
taken excessive liberties or to have misunderstood the originals, were in
many cases actually right on the mark; it is we moderns who did not
understand and are only now beginning to catch up with them."[11]
Sahagún was sensitive to the difficulties of his undertaking and fearful
that a European audience would not accept the legitimacy of the
huehuehtlahtolli: "what is written in this book is impossible for the human mind to invent, nor could any man living invent the language it is
in. And all educated Indians, if they were asked, would affirm that this
is the authentic language of their ancestors and the works they composed."[12]

In addition to the speeches preserved by Sahagún there are a few
other major collections of *huehuehtlahtolli.* The most important of these
are the speeches collected by Andrés de Olmos and translated into Spanish by Juan Bautista as *Huehuetlahtolli o pláticas de los viejos* (1600).[13] Olmos
(ca. 1491–1570 or 1571) probably preceded Sahagún as a collector of
huehuehtlahtolli and so shares with Fray Bernardino the credit for developing an ethnographic method for eliciting and recording the discourse
of the other. Olmos gathered his collection of *huehuehtlahtolli* between
1540 and 1545. He also wrote the first surviving Nahuatl grammar, *Arte
de la lengua mexicana,* to which the "Speeches of the Ancients" was ap-

pended in 1547.[14] Some, but not all, of the surviving manuscripts of his *Arte* include the *huehuehtlahtolli*.[15] The relationship between the work of Olmos and Sahagún is not entirely clear, but it may well be that Olmos established the methodology, including the systematic interrogation of Indian informants, used by Sahagún so profitably in the *General History*.[16]

Two other important sources of *huehuehtlahtolli* include the addresses probably gathered by Horacio Carochi in the seventeenth century and published in 1892 under the title "Arte de la lengua mexicana"[17] and the "Bancroft Dialogues," which may also have been collected by Carochi.[18] In addition to these collections of *huehuehtlahtolli* the speeches also appear in many of the sixteenth- and seventeenth-century chronicles of New Spain, including Alonso de Zurita's *Brief and Summary Relation of the Lords of New Spain* (ca. 1570)[19] and Juan de Torquemada's *Monarquía Indiana* (1615).[20]

Book 6 of the *General History*, "Rhetoric and Moral Philosophy," remains the most cornucopian source of *huehuehtlahtolli*. In this book, says Sahagún, "are told the various words of prayer with which they prayed to those who were their gods; and how they made formal conversation through which they displayed rhetoric and moral philosophy, as is evident in the discourses."[21] Sahagún then presents the text of sixty *huehuehtlahtolli*; another twenty-six are scattered throughout the other eleven books of the *General History*.

Despite considerable variety among the *huehuehtlahtolli*, certain patterns of discourse do emerge from Sahagún's texts. Thelma Sullivan suggests that the speeches compiled by Sahagún may be divided into five categories.[22] The first of these categories is composed of twelve prayers to the gods. These speeches, usually delivered by priests, most often take the form of supplications directed to capricious deities. A second category consists of court orations, addresses given by nobles or kings at a variety of state functions. A third category of *huehuehtlahtolli* are those orations given by parents to their offspring on the subject of appropriate behavior in society. The orations of the merchants constitute the fourth category of speeches. These addresses were given by the elders of the commercial community to mark the departure and return of trading expeditions. The final, and most numerous, category consists of orations relative to the life cycle. These speeches were delivered by elders or parents at crucial junctures in human experience: birth, infancy, marriage, and death.

Naturally, such an anthology of speeches represent a great repository of information regarding the thought and culture of the Mexicas. Indeed, Alfredo López Austin maintains that "for those trying to gain an acquaintance with the people of ancient Mexico, whether in the sphere of ethnohistory or that of literature or of the broadest humanism, no other book among the twelve has the value of the sixth book."[23] Certainly, the *huehuehtlahtolli* have contributed significantly to the historical understanding of the Mexicas. One feature of this understanding which is rarely emphasized by historians is the great importance of public discourse in the religious, political, and social aspects of Mexica life.[24] The speeches invariably reflect occasions of extreme ritualistic and ceremonial moment.

Not surprisingly, orations of such religious and political import were not the products of spontaneous utterance. The *huehuehtlahtolli* were, rather, carefully crafted discourses delivered by men who had been formally trained in the art of public speaking. The sons of Aztec nobility attended the *calmecac,* the institution for the training of religious and civil functionaries. The curriculum of the *calmecac* included the arts of public speaking and civil conversation. "Very carefully," says Sahagún, "were they taught good discourse. If one spoke not well, if one greeted others not well, then they drew blood from him [with maguey spines]."[25]

Although Sahagún does not specify the methods employed by the priests to teach "good discourse," other sources indicate that the students memorized speeches transmitted orally from previous generations. Francisco Javier Clavijero, in his *Historia antigua de Mexico,* maintains that "those who were destined to be orators were instructed from childhood to speak well, and they made them learn from memory the most famous speeches of their ancestors, which had been passed down from fathers to sons."[26] Despite this fidelity to ancestral addresses, Mexica orators must also have created original orations derived from traditional themes and commonplaces when confronted with new situations or exigencies. The most obvious example of such an exigency is Montezuma II's speech welcoming Cortés to Tenochtitlán.[27] There is, however, little, if any, evidence to indicate that rhetorical composition was taught formally to young Mexica orators. Indeed, the emphasis in the *calmecac,* as in the public ceremonies, was almost certainly upon the careful transmission of previously developed discourse.

The youth of the *calmecac* would eventually become the orators responsible for inculcating and perpetuating the accumulated wisdom of the ages. The oratory thus transmitted is characterized by what Robert T. Oliver calls the "rhetoric of behavior": language intended to induce individual conformity to traditional values.[28] While appropriate behavior is an essential theme of most *huehuehtlahtolli,* such concerns are especially apparent in the speeches of parents addressing their children. In one such speech a father advises his son on the virtues of chastity. The father begins: "Thou who art my son, thou who art my youth, hear the words; place, inscribe in the chambers of thy heart the word or two which our forefathers departed leave: the old men, the old women, the regarded ones, the admired ones, and the advised ones on earth. Here is that which they gave us, entrusted to us as they left, the words of the old men, that which is bound, the well-guarded [words]."[29] With these "well-guarded words" the speaker instructs the boy in the appropriate behavior. "Listen to the way in which thou art to live," says the father. "Thou art not to lust for vice, for filth; thou art not to take pleasure in that which defileth one, which corrupteth one, that which, it is said, driveth one to excess, which harmeth, destroyeth one: that which is deadly."[30] Moreover, the father cautions, "thou art not to ruin thyself impetuously; thou art not to devour, to gulp down the carnal life as if thou wert a dog."[31] Finally, the speech concludes: "And this, O my son: be very careful on earth. Live very calmly, very carefully" (7:119).[32] Admonitions to be chaste, cautious, and moderate are the commonplaces of Mexica oratory.

In another parental address a father exhorts his son to behave prudently in public. One must be careful to dress with modesty, to eat and drink in moderation, to walk with dignity, and "to speak very slowly, very deliberately; thou art not to speak hurriedly, not to pant, nor to squeak, lest it be said of thee that thou art a groaner, a growler, a squeaker. Also thou art not to cry out, lest thou be known as an imbecile, a shameless one, a rustic, very much a rustic. Moderately, middlingly art thou to carry, to emit thy spirit, thy words. And thou art to improve, to soften thy words, thy voice."[33] The father closes with what is perhaps the quintessential admonition of Mexica morality: "Continue with caution on earth, for thou has heard that moderation is necessary."[34]

Despite the recurrent exhortations to moderation, the *huehuehtlahtolli* indicate that the Mexicas did sometimes behave immoderately. One of the longest orations Sahagún includes in book 6 is that of a king addressing the nobility on the subject of the evils of *octli,* the fermented sap of the maguey cactus. The king warns that "what is called *octli* is the origin, the root of the evil, or the bad, of perdition. . . . It is like a whirlwind, like a severe wind, for it cometh rolling together the bad, the evil.

Behold: one [desireth] another's woman; one committeth adultery; one coveteth, one stealeth, one pilfereth; one becometh a snatcher. Behold: it is one who curseth, who murmureth, who belloweth, who rumbleth when he becometh drunk. [Because of] the pulque he braggeth falsely of his noble lineage; he thinketh himself superior; he vaunteth himself; he esteemeth himself; he is grandiose; he regardeth no one with much consideration."[35] "I cry out especially to you," says the king, "ye who are lords, and ye who are our uncles, ye who are noblemen, ye who are the sons of rulers, that we leave alone the jimson weed, which maketh one drunk, confoundeth one; the pulque, which is evil, bad. These who went leaving you, those from whom ye descended, went hating, went detesting it."[36] Thus, temperance, another manifestation of moderation, was much admired by the Mexica's ancestors, an attitude that should be emulated by this present generation.

While many *huehuehtlahtolli,* then, advocate specific behavior, other speeches are designed to inculcate beliefs advantageous to the ruling elite of Mexica society. One such address delivered, according to Sahagún, by "a great priest, or a great nobleman, or some great dignitary" upon the selection of a new ruler seeks to reinforce the legitimacy of the accession. The speaker tells the new leader: "It is thou: he pointeth the finger at thee; he indicateth thee. Our lord hath recorded these, indicated thee, marked thee, entered thee in the books. Now verily it was declared, it was determined above us, in the heavens, in the land of the dead, that our lord place thee on the reed mat, on the reed seat, on his place of honor."[37] This fundamental message is repeated throughout the speech. Once again the speaker says: "It is thou. Upon thee it hath fallen. Upon thee hath gone the spirit, the word of our lord, the lord of the near, of the nigh; he hath pointed his finger at thee. Verily, wilt thou hide thyself? Wilt thou take refuge? Wilt thou be absent? Wilt thou flee? And wilt thou already steel thyself?"[38] Of course, the ruler will accept his responsibility to lead, just as the common people will accept their responsibility to follow. After all, the accession has been determined by the gods and endorsed by the elders; there is no choice.

The Ancient Word and Ancient Rhetoric

Sahagún, introducing the *huehuehtlahtolli* in his *General History,* observes that all nations "have looked to the learned and powerful to persuade, and to men eminent in moral virtues." There are examples of such men "among the Greeks and Romans, Spanish, French and Italians." Also among the Aztecs "learned, virtuous, and enterprising rhetoricians were held in high esteem, and they elected high priests, lords, chiefs, and captains from among them, however low their destiny may have been. These ruled the republic and led the armies, and presided over the temples."[39] Sahagún is clearly identifying the speakers of the ancient word of Mesoamerica with the ancient European rhetorical tradition. In particular, Sahagún is equating the "learned, virtuous, enterprising" (and indigenous) rhetoricians with the Renaissance image of the orator as a cultural idea. Moreover, despite the increasing importance of printing, the oration retained much of its ancient ethos and its normative power over the written word.[40] That oratory, an art so persistently important in European politics and religion, occupied a comparable position in Mexica society must have been very reassuring to Sahagún. So ingrained was the rhetorical tradition in Renaissance education and culture that its practice by the natives of the New World could only be a sign of the civilized status of these peoples. Sahagún's careful preservation of the speeches of the ancients indicates a genuine admiration of Mexica oratory and a conviction that these speeches not only reveal the native mind but also represent a point of mutual contact between two worlds, which appeared to have so few shared traditions.

Sahagún was particularly impressed with the highly figurative quality of the speeches of the ancients. In his headnotes to the speeches Sahagún observes, in one instance, that the "words are very admirable and the metaphors are very difficult." In describing another speech, he notes that "many similes and examples are given expression."[41] Olmos, too, was sufficiently impressed with the figurative nature of the *huehuehtlahtolli* that he included samples of the "metaphors" extracted from the discourses in some manuscripts of his *Arte de la aprender la lengua mexicana*.[42] This collection of metaphors, according to Maxwell and Hanson, "illustrated literary tropes common to Aztec courtly speech and provided missionaries with building blocks to communicate Christian theology through indigenous images."[43]

Sahagún and Olmos, by focusing on the metaphors in the *huehuehtlahtolli*, follow the rhetorical tradition of making the mastery of tropes a key aspect of eloquence. From its inception European rhetoric had valued figurative language, and this appreciation was especially acute in the Renaissance. Granada, in a manner typical of many Renaissance treatises, devoted considerably more of the *Ecclesiasticae rhetoricae* to *elocutio,* including the tropes and figures, than he did any of the other traditional parts of rhetoric. That the Mexica were so highly developed in the figurative and the tropological can hardly have escaped Sahagún's notice as a sign of congruence with European assumptions about the importance of figurative language.

Like Sahagún and Olmos, modern readers are also struck by the multiplicity of metaphors in the speeches of the ancients. The highly figurative quality of these speeches leads Charles E. Dibble to conclude that "the Aztecs conceived of their orations and prayers as the stringing of a strand of beads and the *huehuetlahtolli* is just that—a series of metaphors one after another."[44] Indeed, metaphoric profusion appears to be a fundamental feature of the Nahuatl language. In the *huehuehtlahtolli,* as in most Mexica literature, the metaphors are almost invariably paired—that is, two similar and consecutive metaphors appear in the same sentence to convey the same thought. In his *Historia de la literature Nahuatl* Angel Maria Garibay K. identifies this metaphoric pairing as *difrasismo.*[45] Examples of "diphrasis" are provided in the speech Sahagún identifies as containing many "very difficult" metaphors: a speech delivered at the inauguration of a new leader. Before the leader can be honored, however, the death of the previous ruler must be dealt with. The orator wonders if the departed ancestors have forgotten those who remain on earth. "Do they," he asks, "still know of their city, which already lieth abandoned, which already lieth darkened, which our lord hath already made his place of desolation? Do they still frequent that which is already completely forest, which is already completely desert, where the governed go? And the vassals no longer possess a mother, no longer possess a father."[46] In three sentences the speaker has presented three paired metaphors. The ruler's death has left the city "darkened" and "abandoned," a "forest" and a "desert." Moreover, his death has deprived the commoners of both a "mother" and a "father." Here, then, is a "strand of beads," an accumulation of metaphors to express and symbolize, to repeat and reinforce, an essential ideal.

This metaphoric abundance appears again and again in the texts preserved by Sahagún. Despite the diversity of subject matter, these speeches share certain essential stylistic and situational elements. The *huehuehtlahtolli* are invariably exhortative and admonitive, poetic and metaphoric. Above all, however, they are the ancient word: the orators inevitably invoke the authority of the dead to assure the accord of the living.

Sahagún was impressed not only by the figurative language of the *huehuehtlahtolli* but also by the highly moralistic message of these orations. This combination of artifice and ethics in the *huehuehtlahtolli* would almost certainly have caused Sahagún to think of epideictic oratory—the classical rhetorical genus that is highly developed in Renaissance theories of rhetoric.[47] John W. O'Malley explains that epideictic oratory was, in general, "intended for a ceremonial occasion, and its purpose was to arouse the sentiments of appreciation or disgust appropriate for some given person, event, or institution. Its characteristic technique was the distribution of praise or blame as circumstances required. It was the *ars laudandi et vituperandi,* the rhetoric of congratulation and the rhetoric of reproach."[48] Cypriano Soarez, in his *De arte rhetorica* (1586), enumerates the merits of epideictic speaking: "there is no style of oratory which can be a more copious source of speaking, more serviceable to governments, or one in which an orator is more engaged in learning to know virtues and vices."[49]

It is this attention to virtue and vice which must have attracted Sahagún to the *huehuehtlahtolli,* and it is this same ethical imperative that links them to the epideictic oratory of Europe. Ethics was a recurrent concern of Sahagún's, and the *huehuehtlahtolli* offer extraordinary insight into indigenous moralizing. As Sahagún says in the beginning of book 6 of the *General History,* it is through these speeches that the Mexica displayed their "moral philosophy." This alliance of rhetoric and ethics, argues Brian Vickers, helps account for the dominance of the epideictic genre in the Renaissance: "rhetoric had aligned itself with philosophy, especially with ethics, so that the poet, like the orator, became the propagator of accepted moral systems."[50] In the *huehuehtlahtolli* the speakers, the elders, were most assuredly propagators of an accepted moral system.

Despite this link between ethics and epideictic, the genus has often been deprecated because of the propensity of skillful orators to employ its conventions for ostentatious display. This criticism of epideictic as display is perhaps only partially justified. The performance element of such rhetoric, says Kenneth Burke, "was merely an extreme expression of a tendency present in epideictic at the start. For this kind contained the most essential motive of all: persuasion by words, rather than by force, on the part of those who loved eloquence for itself alone. Critics must have epideictic in mind who say that eloquence begins in the love of words for their own sake."[51] The Mexica, despite their moments of ferocity, were also lovers of words—people who were compelled to speak out at times of public and private significance.

Huehuehtlahtolli and the Origins of Rhetoric

Both Mexica and Europeans shared a belief in the efficacy of the spoken word and an appreciation of the artistry of its expression. By their civic and ceremonial functions and the elegance of their language, Sahagún recognized the *huehuehtlahtolli* as rhetoric. Yet, despite the apparent parallels between the *huehuehtlahtolli* and classical rhetoric, the speeches of the ancients are not the orations of European courts and cathedrals, and Sahagún does not claim that they are. The speeches of the ancients differ thematically, structurally, and stylistically from European oratory. The oratory of the Mexica is typically brief, aphoristic, and repetitive. Indeed, the dominant form of the ancient word might be described as constant repetition made palatable by metaphoric variety. In short, the *huehuehtlahtolli* possess many of the characteristics that constitute what Walter Ong calls the "psycho-dynamics orality." In particular, Mexica oratory is structurally additive rather than subordinative, stylistically copious and redundant and thematically conservative.[52] Sahagún's collection demonstrates that the *huehuehtlahtolli*, while resembling European oratory in many ways, also differ from it in significant respects. These differences offer great potential for understanding what elements of rhetoric may transcend the European origins of the art.

"One of the objectives of the historical study of rhetoric," says George Kennedy, "is to come to an understanding of the common ground of rhetoric and to see what may be universal and what may be historical accident." Kennedy further observes that "in an attempt to define the nature of rhetoric and its historical manifestations we are fortunate in having on record descriptions of the circumstances and contents of speeches that were composed before the conceptualization of rhetoric. Such records exist in India and China, and in the West are represented in their most remarkable form by the Homeric poems in Greece and by the Old Testament."[53]

Historians of rhetoric are also fortunate to have the *huehuehtlahtolli* collected and preserved by Sahagún and his collaborators. These speeches of the ancients suggest that the art of rhetoric originated in the early rituals of humankind. Virtually all the speeches presented by Sahagún were delivered on ceremonial occasions—moments that were of great importance to the Mexica, "an inordinately ritualistic and ceremonial people."[54]

Such an inference about the origins of rhetoric is not altogether inconsistent with the experience of the early Greeks. Although ancient theory was preoccupied with the forensic oratory necessitated by the Athenian popular jury, ancient practice was also greatly concerned with ceremonial oratory. The public funerals, festivals, and games of Athenian life were typically accompanied by the exercise of epideictic oratory. And many of the great early practitioners of rhetoric were masters of epideictic; Pericles, Gorgias, and Isocrates all excelled in this genre. After the demise of Athenian democracy epideictic displayed a remarkable durability and adaptability. This persistence is no doubt due, in part, to the relative independence of epideictic, in contrast to forensic and deliberative, from the institutional requirements imposed by the courtroom and the assembly chamber. But the persistence of epideictic must also be a product of its fundamental association with human behavior. The Mexica penchant for ceremonial oratory serves as a reminder of the fundamental necessity, shared by oral and literate cultures alike, of exhorting and admonishing, of praising and blaming, of moralizing through language.

Historians have long valued Sahagún's collection of speeches for the ethnographic data they provide about Mexica thought and culture. The *huehuehtlahtolli* are also vitally important for the information they impart about the role of rhetoric not only in the Mexica world but in oral societies generally. The speeches of the ancients, delivered by a complex and ritualistic people, represent one of the most extensive collections of the oratory of any ancient non-European culture. When recorded by Sahagún, the Mexica had been in contact with Europeans for barely three decades. Thus, Sahagún's texts make possible the observation of the rhetoric of a sophisticated oral culture in a form relatively unaltered by the intervention of a literate, colonial culture. Sahagún seized an opportunity that would never present itself again. It is probable that Mexica discourse, both practically and conceptually, would have continued to evolve as the culture itself developed. Such a development was, of course, irrevocably interrupted by Cortés. The *huehuehtlahtolli* are, therefore, not only the words of the ancients but also virtually the last words of the Mexica.

Bernardino de Sahagún's collection of *huehuehtlahtolli* in the *General History of the Things of New Spain* is an invaluable contribution to the historical understanding of the Mexica people and culture. The "Rhetoric and Moral Philosophy" of the Mexica is equally significant as an extraordinary repository of the oratory of indigenous Mesoamericans. Beyond all that Sahagún's compilation conveys about the Mexica, the *huehuehtlahtolli* also advances the effort to identify those elements of rhetoric which may transcend the exigencies of a particular society and reflect the wider needs of humanity. The ethical admonitions so apparent in the speeches of the ancients provide additional evidence of the universality of the epideictic genre. Indeed, the *huehuehtlahtolli* offer eloquent testimony to rhetoric's fundamental role as a moralizing force in both the Old World and the New.

Notes

1. The Christianization of the New World was initially undertaken by the Mendicant orders: the Franciscans, the Dominicans, and the Augustinians. The Franciscans arrived first in New Spain and dominated the missionary effort in the sixteenth century. See Robert Ricard, *The Spiritual Conquest of Mexico: An Essay on the Apostolate and the Evangelizing Methods of the Mendicant Orders of New Spain, 1523–1572*, trans. Lesley Bird Simpson (Berkeley: University of California Press, 1966); and Pius J. Barth, *Franciscan Education and the Social Order in Spanish North America (1502–1821)* (Ph.D. diss., University of Chicago, 1945).

2. "Sahagún and the Birth of Modern Ethnography: Representing, Confessing, and Inscribing the Native Other," in *The Work of Bernardino de Sahagún: Pioneer Ethnographer of Sixteenth-Century Aztec Mexico*, ed. J. Jorge Klor de Alva, H. B. Nicholson, and Eloise Quiñones Keber (Albany: Institute for Mesoamerican Studies, 1988), 35. Luis Nicolau D'Olwer had also credited Sahagún with the creation of "ethnographic investigation" (*Fray Bernardino de Sahagún* [Mexico City: Instituto Panamericano de Geografía e Historia, 1952], 135–42).

3. "The Rhetorical Orations, or *Huehuetlahtolli*, Collected by Sahagún," in *Sixteenth-Century Mexico: The Work of Sahagún*, ed. Munro S. Edmundson (Albuquerque: University of New Mexico Press, 1974), 82.

4. Biographical details are provided by D'Olwer, *Fray Bernardino de Sahagún*. Especially helpful is the "Chronological Index," 199–204.

5. For a bibliography of Sahagún's work, including archival locations, see Edmundson, *Sixteenth-Century Mexico*, 268–71.

6. Except where otherwise noted, I have relied upon the following edition of Sahagún's work: *Florentine Codex: General History of the Things of New Spain*, trans. Arthur J. O. Anderson and Charles Dibble, 12 pts. (Santa Fe, N.M.: School of American Research and University of Utah, 1950–69).

7. *Aztecs: An Interpretation* (Cambridge: Cambridge University Press, 1991), 279. This statement appears in "A Question of Sources" (277–93), a very useful summary of the difficulties of interpreting sixteenth-century texts.

8. Ibid., 283.

9. Anderson and Dibble, "Temporary Foreword," in Sahagún, *Florentine Codex*, pt. 2.

10. The problems attendant to such a process are explored in Rosanna Warren, ed., *The Art of Translation: Voices from the Field* (Boston: Northeastern University Press), 1989. See esp. Jorge Klor de Alva, "Language, Politics, and Translation: Colonial Discourse and Classical Nahuatl in New Spain," 143–62.

11. "Preliminary Study," *The Art of Nahuatl Speech: The Bancroft Dialogues* (Los Angeles: UCLA Latin American Center, 1987), 17.

12. "Prologo," Libro Sexto, *Historia general de las cosas de Nueva España*, ed. Angel Maria Garibay K., 5 vols. (Mexico City: Editorial Porrúa, 1956), 2:53. The *Florentine Codex* does not include this prologue. The Spanish edition quoted here, however, also uses material from the other manuscripts, the "Madrid Codices" of the *Biblioteca del Palacio* and the *Academia de la Historia*, Madrid.

13. Juan Bautista, *Huehuetlahtolli* (Mexico City, ca. 1600), rpt. in vol. 3, *Colección de documentos para la historia mexicana*, ed. Antonio Peñafiel (Mexico City: Secretaría de Fomento, 1901); *Huehuehtlatolli: Testimonios de la antigua palabra*, intro. Miguel León Portilla, trans. Librado Silva Galeana (from Nahuatl) (Mexico City: Secretaría de Educacion Publica, 1991; Judith M. Maxwell and Craig A. Hanson, *Of the Manners of Speaking That the Old Ones Had: The Metaphors of Andrés de Olmos in the TULAL Manuscript* (Salt Lake City: University of Utah Press, 1992). While this latter work does not include the *huehuehtlatolli*, it does present the "metaphors" that Olmos offered, together with the *huehuehtlatolli*, as evidence of the elegant expression of the Mexica.

14. S. Jeffrey K. Wilkerson, "The Ethnographic Work of Andrés de Olmos, Precursor and Contemporary of Sahagún," *Sixteenth-Century Mexico*, 65.

15. For a summary of these manuscripts, see Maxwell and Hanson, *Of the Manners of Speaking*, 10–19.

16. Wilkerson, "Ethnographic Work," 74.

17. *Arte de la lengua mexicana: con la de declaración de los adverbios della: edición facsimilar de la publicada por Juan Ruyz en la Cuidad de México, 1645*, intro. Miguel León-Portilla (Mexico City: Universidad Nacional Autonoma de México, 1983).

18. *The Art of Nahautl Speech: The Bancroft Dialogues*, ed. Frances Kartunen and James Lockhart. These dialogues may have served as instructional material for Jesuits studying with Carochi. See "Preliminary Study," 2–3.

19. Ed. and trans. Benjamin Keen (New Brunswick, N.J.: Rutgers University Press, 1963), 97–102 and 140–51.

20. Ed. Miguel León-Portilla (Mexico City: Editorial Porrúa, 1969), 2:492–99.

21. *Florentine Codex*, 7:1.

22. Sullivan, "Rhetorical Orations," 85–107.

23. "The Research Methods of Fray Bernardino de Sahagún: The Question-naires," *Sixteenth-Century Mexico*, 133.

24. The most obvious feature of the *huehuetlahtolli*—that they are, quite simply, speeches—is often overlooked by historians in search of other ethnographic data. Even when the *huehuetlahtolli* are considered as literature, their oratorical origin is often obscured. A notable exception to such approaches is Sullivan who, in "The Rhetorical Orations," does consider these discourses as oratory.

25. *Florentine Codex*, 4:64–65.

26. (Mexico City: Editorial Porrúa, 1958), 2:273.

27. *Florentine Codex*, 13:41–43.

28. *Communication and Culture in Ancient India and China* (Syracuse, N.Y.: Syracuse University Press, 1971), chap. 9, "The Rhetoric of Behavior: Ceremony, Etiquette, and Methodology," 145–60. Although Oliver is not, of course, discussing Aztec culture, the parallels between his subject and the *huehuetlahtolli* are striking: "Rhetoric in Chinese Society thus came to be very much akin to sheer propriety. The utility which rhetoric was to serve was the maintenance of harmony. The way to this goal was through ceremony, etiquette, and methodology. There was a right way of doing things—a way that was established and accepted. When behavior conformed to this pattern of expectation, the individual's relations with his fellows would be predictable and dependable. Accordingly, the community would have a decent and decorous stability" (145).

29. *Florentine Codex*, 7:113.

30. Ibid., 7:116.

31. Ibid.

32. Ibid., 7:119.

33. Ibid., 7:122.

34. Ibid., 7:126.

35. Ibid., 7:68.

36. Ibid., 7:70.

37. Ibid., 7:48.

38. Ibid., 7:49.

39. *Historia general de las cosas de Nueva España* (1956), 2:53.

40. The dominance of oratorical forms in the Renaissance leads Walter Ong to claim that the oration "tyrannized over ideas of what expression as such—literary or other—was" ("Tudor Writings on Rhetoric, Poetic, and Literary Theory," in *Rhetoric, Romance, and Technology: Studies in the Interaction of Expression and Culture* [Ithaca: Cornell University Press, 1971], 53). See also Don Paul Abbott, "Rhetoric and Writing in Renaissance Europe and England," in *A Short History of Writing Instruction: From Ancient Greece to Twentieth-Century America*, ed. James J. Murphy (Davis, Calif.: Hermagoras Press, 1990), 106–9.

41. *Florentine Codex,* 7:47, 113.

42. The metaphors appear in three of the six surviving manuscripts of the *Arte;* each manuscript contains a different number of tropes: 102, 62, and 50. The examples presented by Olmos are not necessarily metaphors in a strict sense: "The word *metáfora* does not appear in the manuscript. The Spanish introduction to the section of the Olmos manuscript analyzed here refers to the examples it gives as samples of 'the old ones' manners of speaking . . . ancient colloquies.' The introduction further notes that these 'manners of speaking' are 'metaphorical' because the literal sense implies one thing and yet the passages often mean quite another. We have denominated these passages 'Metaphors'" (Maxwell and Hanson, *Of the Manners of Speaking,* 19).

43. Ibid., 1.

44. "The Nahuatlization of Christianity," *Sixteenth-Century Mexico,* 228.

45. (Mexico City: Editorial Porrúa, 1953) 1:19–20. See also the same author's *Llave del Nahuatl* (Mexico City: Editorial Porrúa, 1961), 115–16. In both these works Garibay K. identifies *difrasismo* as a fundamental feature of the Nahuatl language.

46. *Florentine Codex,* 7:47.

47. For the importance of the epideictic genre in the Renaissance, see O. B. Hardison Jr., *The Enduring Monument: A Study of the Idea of Praise in Renaissance Literary Theory and Practice* (Chapel Hill: University of North Carolina Press, 1962); and Brian Vickers, "Epideictic and Epic in the Renaissance," *New Literary History* 14 (1982): 497–537.

48. *Praise and Blame in Renaissance Rome* (Durham: Duke University Press, 1979), 39.

49. Trans. Lawrence J. Flynn, S.J. (Ph.D. diss., University of Florida, 1955), 183.

50. "Epideictic and Epic in the Renaissance," 502.

51. *A Rhetoric of Motives* (Berkeley: University of California Press, 1969), 71–72.

52. *Orality and Literacy: The Technologizing of the Word* (London and New York: Methuen, 1982), 31–77.

53. *Classical Rhetoric and Its Christian and Secular Tradition from Ancient to Modern Times* (Chapel Hill: University of North Carolina Press, 1980), 8–9.

54. Sullivan, "Rhetorical Orations," 109.

Chapter 3

Diego Valadés
An Ancient Art in a New World

Bernardino de Sahagún represents the first generation of the Franciscan evangelical mission to the New World; Diego Valadés belongs to the second generation of the order's missionaries in Mexico. Sahagún listened to the speeches of the ancients and recognized them as rhetoric. Valadés, on the other hand, embraced the rhetorical tradition of ancient Greece and Rome as a means of Christianizing the natives of New Spain. His *Rhetorica Christiana* (1579) represents the first comprehensive rhetoric that both is cognizant of the existence of peoples other than Europeans and attempts to understand how one might communicate with such people.[1] Whereas Sahagún's *General History* is a narrative of the Mexicas' customs, including their public discourse, Valadés's *Rhetorica Christiana* is a rhetoric in the European tradition which reports on life in the Valley of Mexico. For Valadés ethnographic observation is secondary to rhetorical precept. The *Rhetorica Christiana* is a book, then, that resembles in important ways both Granada's *Rhetoricae Ecclesiasticae* and Sahagún's *General History*.

The *Rhetorica Christiana* is an extraordinary combination of Old World erudition and New World anthropology. In its pages Valadés transmits the literature of the Greeks and Romans and records the customs of the Mexica and the Chichimecas. The *Rhetorica Christiana*, while very much a product of European humanism, is not an entirely conventional rhetoric of its time. It is a treatise that departs in significant ways from the accepted norms of Renaissance rhetoric. When Valadés deviates from the dominant idiom of sixteenth-century rhetoric, he does so, almost invariably, because of his life as a teacher and preacher in the New World. Thus, many of the distinctive features of Valadés's rhetorical theory derive from his mastery of European erudition, his understanding of Amerindian culture, and his attempt to integrate the two into a coherent theory of rhetoric. The *Rhetorica Christiana*, then, conceived in Mexico and written in Europe, represents the recognition that the rhetorical tradition must transcend the boundaries of the Old World.

Diego Valadés: Missionary in His Own Land

Diego Valadés was born in the New World, and his *Rhetorica Christiana* is almost certainly the first book written by a native of Mexico to be published in Europe. Perhaps more than any other Renaissance rhetoric, the *Rhetorica Christiana* is as much the memoirs of a man's life as it is a rhetorical treatise. Valadés was born in 1533 in the city of Tlaxcala, east of the Mexica capital of Tenochtitlán. His father, also called Diego Valadés, was a conquistador who had arrived in New Spain in 1520 with the expedition of Pánfilo de Narváez. The conquistador's father, Alonso Valadés, had fought the Moors in the Spanish war of reconquest. Thus, the Valadés family had a long tradition of converting nonbelievers, a tradition the younger Diego would continue in more peaceful ways. Diego's mother was a now anonymous Tlaxcalan Indian. There is no convincing evidence to indicate that the birth was other than illegitimate.

At an early age Valadés came under the tutelage of Pedro de Gante, or Peter of Ghent, who is generally regarded as the initiator of European education in New Spain. Gante founded the school of San Francisco in Mexico City, adjacent to the chapel of San José de los Naturales. This institution served as a primary school for the education of Indian children, teaching them reading, writing, arithmetic, music, and fine and practical arts. Instruction was conducted almost exclusively in Nahuatl using the Latin alphabet, rather than pictographs, as the written basis of the language. While liturgical Latin was also taught, it apparently did not serve as a language of daily instruction. It is likely that Valadés received his primary education at Pedro de Gante's school for Indian elite. In the *Rhetorica Christiana* Valadés praises the Flemish friar as "a man of singular religion and piety, who taught the Indians all the arts; he was ignorant of none of them."[2]

The young Valadés must have attracted the attention of his Franciscan teachers, for he was admitted to the order sometime during the years 1548 to 1550. The Franciscan authorities in New Spain presumably suppressed the illegitimacy of his birth and his mixed parentage from the order's hierarchy in Europe. For, although the early Franciscan missionaries were committed to a native clergy, there was

considerable opposition from other elements of the church to the ordi-
nation of Mexican priests. Valadés was one of a very small number of
mestizos allowed to enter religious orders before such entrance was prohibited by official policy. The synod of 1555 formally forbade the ordi-
nation of mestizos, Indians, and "Negroes."[3] This policy of excluding
natives from the clergy would have significant consequences for the
church, ensuring that it would be governed by a colonial, rather than a
Mexican, hierarchy. As Robert Ricard concludes, "this error prevented
the Church from striking deep roots in the nation, gave it the appearance and character of a foreign institution, and kept it strictly depen-
dent on the mother country."[4] Thus, Valadés, as a mestizo, occupied an
exceptional position in the church in New Spain and in Europe.

After joining the Franciscans, Valadés presumably continued his
education in one of the order's educational institutions; most likely at
the Colegio de Santa Cruz de Tlaltelolco. Founded by the Franciscans in
1536 to provide humanistic education to the sons of caciques, this *colegio*
may well be considered the first European institution of higher education in North America. The first professors were the elite of the Franciscan
missionaries; these were later joined by natives who had themselves
been trained at Tlaltelolco. The curriculum was an approximation of
Renaissance education: grammar, logic, rhetoric, philosophy, and music, together with the herbal medicine of the Mexica. Rhetoric, as well as
philosophy, was taught by Fray Juan de Gaona, who had been educated
in Paris. It appears probable, then, that the first students of rhetoric in
the New World were natives of that world. The University of Mexico, an
institution devoted to educating the sons of Spaniards, was founded in
1553, nearly two decades after the college at Santa Cruz. The teaching of
rhetoric at the university began on 12 July 1553 under the professorship
of Francisco Cervantes de Salazar.[5]

The library at Tlaltelolco provides a gauge of the extent of European
humanism's penetration into the Valley of Mexico. By 1572 the library
contained some seventy-one volumes, including the following rhetorical works: Cicero's orations and his *De Oratore* as well as Quintilian's
Institutio oratoria. The library at Tlaltelolco also included works by such
ancient authors as Aristotle, Plato, Martial, Juvenal, Virgil, and Livy and
Renaissance works by Erasmus, Juan Luis Vives, and Antonio de Nebrija.
Tlaltelolco also possessed at least one book of Mexican origin: Fray
Alonso de Molina's study of the Nahuatl language, *Diccionario en
castellano y mexicano*.[6]

Clearly, the intent of the *colegio* was to educate the sons of native nobility in a manner comparable to the education available to the children of privileged Europeans. In this ambitious undertaking the Franciscans were at least partially successful. In his chronicle Cervantes de Salazar, the Dominican professor of rhetoric at the University of Mexico, mentions a "college for the Indians, who are taught to speak and write in Latin. They have a teacher of their own nationality, Antonio Valeriano, who is in no respect inferior to our own grammarians. He is well trained in the observance of Christian law and is an ardent student of oratory."[7] Another contemporary Spanish source admitted that Valeriano "spoke Latin with such propriety and elegance that he equalled Cicero or Quintilian."[8] In Mexico, as in Europe, comparisons with the ancients were inevitable and essential.

It is difficult to know just how many of the Indian's students' latinity really rivaled Cicero, but Valadés's *Rhetorica Christiana* provides evidence that the Franciscans' system was capable of creating true humanistic scholars. While Valadés is, of course, exceptional, the *colegio* did train a generation of copyists and translators, who proved to be valuable collaborators in the effort to Christianize the indigenous population.[9] The college at Tlaltelolco was, however, greatly vitiated by the civil and ecclesiastical opposition to a native clergy, an opposition that would ultimately deprive the *colegio* of its reason for being. In the mid-sixteenth century the *colegio* entered a period of decline, and in 1576 the student body was decimated by the plague. In the early seventeenth century the college was reduced to an elementary school. Eighteenth-century proposals to revitalize the school were never realized, and the *colegio* and its buildings at Santa Cruz de Tlaltelolco slowly disintegrated.

In its early years, at least, the *colegio* demonstrated the possibilities of replicating Renaissance learning in the Valley of Mexico. The *colegio* was predicated upon the conviction that the education of the natives should correspond as closely as possible to the humanistic curriculum. While this educational experimentation imposed an almost exclusively European model of learning on native youth, it did nevertheless provide for the intensive schooling of those youths. In the increasingly conservative post-Tridentine climate the education of native children would become progressively untenable.

Valadés was no doubt regarded as an exemplar of the Franciscan educational experiment. His education appears to have completely Europeanized Valadés. Despite his birth and parentage Valadés was as much a missionary as Sahagún. In his writing Valadés never identifies with

the natives; they are always Indians, always the other. With his education completed by about 1556 Valadés would devote many years to his
mission among the natives of New Spain. In the *Rhetorica Christiana* he
remarks that he spent some twenty years preaching and hearing confessions in three native languages: Mexican (Nahuatl), Tarascan, and
Otomi.[10] From 1558 to 1562 he participated in the evangelization of the
nomadic and warlike Chichimecas in the northern frontier provinces of
Durango and Zacatecas. After his return from the north Valadés taught
in Franciscan schools—probably the very ones in which he had been
educated. He likely taught painting and engraving at Gante's school at
San José de los Naturales. Such an assumption is given credence by the
elaborate engravings that illustrate the *Rhetorica Christiana* and are indeed the book's best-known feature.

  After almost forty years in his native Mexico, Valadés was called to
Europe by his order, and in 1571 he left New Spain for old. From 1575 to
1577 he served in Rome as the procurator general of the Franciscan order—a position that combined the duties of a chargé d'affaires, agent,
and attorney. In 1579 Valadés was in Perugia to supervise the printing
of the *Rhetorica Christiana*. The final years of his life were spent in Italy;
he was never to return to Mexico. The probable year of his death was
1582.

The *Rhetorica Christiana*

  Valadés was truly a man of two worlds, the Old and the New, and
the *Rhetorica Christiana* reflects the duality of his life. The world of European humanism is dominant, but the oral world of Valadés's birthplace
is ever present in the *Rhetorica Christiana*. Valadés's mastery of humanism and his understanding of rhetoric is apparent from even a cursory
review of the book. Such a review also reveals that Valadés was not simply a slavish synthesizer of Renaissance humanism but was an able
adapter of humanist thought to the exigencies of the New World. Like
Granada's *Ecclesiasticae rhetoricae*, the *Rhetorica Christiana* was written
after the Council of Trent's call for improved preaching, and so, like
Granada, Valadés's objective was to create the Christian embodiment of
the Ciceronian ideal: an orator who would truly deserve to be identified
as "the good man speaking well."[11]

  The *Rhetorica Christiana* shares much with Granada's *Ecclesiasticae
rhetoricae* and other religious rhetorics of the sixteenth century, yet

Valadés's work cannot be called a typical Renaissance rhetoric. A brief summary of the *Rhetorica Christiana* will convey the scope of Valadés's treatise. It is divided into six parts. Part 1 is devoted to the qualities and properties required to create the Christian orator. In part 2 Valadés defines rhetoric and discusses its constituent parts: invention, disposition, memory, and elocution. All four are discussed briefly, with the exception of memory, which receives a detailed treatment. Part 3 is devoted to an explication of the Scriptures, the primary source of the Christian orator's message. *Pronuntiatio*, which Valadés had earlier omitted as a part of rhetoric, receives detailed attention in this section. Part 3 concludes with a consideration of how to move the sentiments of the audience. Part 4 begins with a discussion of the three genera of oratory: demonstrative, deliberative, and judicial. Following a discussion of demonstrative oratory, Valadés embarks on an account of the natives of the New World. He then returns to the remaining two genera of oratory. This, in turn, is followed by an additional account of indigenous customs and practices. Part 5 treats the structure of a discourse. In the sixth part of the *Rhetorica Christiana* Valadés considers, "as briefly as possible," the figures and tropes. The *Rhetorica Christiana* concludes with Valadés's commentary on the *Book of Sentences* of the twelfth-century theologian Peter Lombard.

The *Rhetorica Christiana*, while attentive to traditional subjects, also contains some obvious departures from the standard rhetorical lore. Indeed, the difference between Valadés and other Renaissance rhetorics is apparent even from the most cursory inspection of the volume. The reader is immediately confronted by a series of elaborate engravings drawn by Valadés himself.[12] Valadés explains that these engravings have not been included simply for the amusement of the reader but, rather, are designed to assist the reader in retaining the content of the *Rhetorica Christiana*.[13] The drawings are an integral part of the book, and their presence in the *Rhetorica Christiana* signals the importance that visual imagery will have in Valadés's conception of rhetoric. These illustrations are the best-known feature of the *Rhetorica Christiana* and have overshadowed Valadés's theory of rhetoric.

The work is distinguished not only by Valadés's engravings but also by his narrative of the natives of New Spain. Much like the illustrations, many of which portray native life, this chronicle of indigenous and colonial customs has obscured the greater portion of the book. Indeed, the *Rhetorica Christiana* is often treated as if it were an account of the Indians with a brief rhetoric appended, when it is more the other way around.

All illustrations are from Diego Valadés,
Rhetorica Christiana (1579)

Title page

The seven liberal arts

Missionary preaching the Passion of Christ to a native audience
with the aid of illustrated screens (*lienzos*)

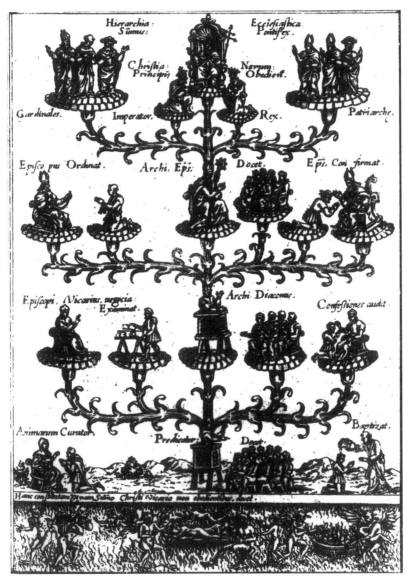

Tree depicting the ecclesiastical hierarchy

Tree depicting the imperial hierarchy

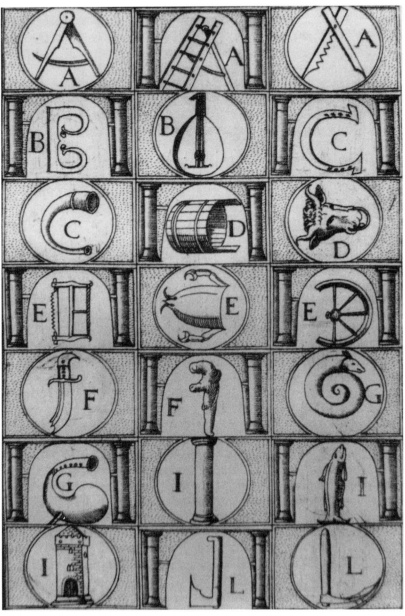

Mnemonic alphabet employing the similarity of shapes between
letters and common objects (derived from Ludovico Dolce)

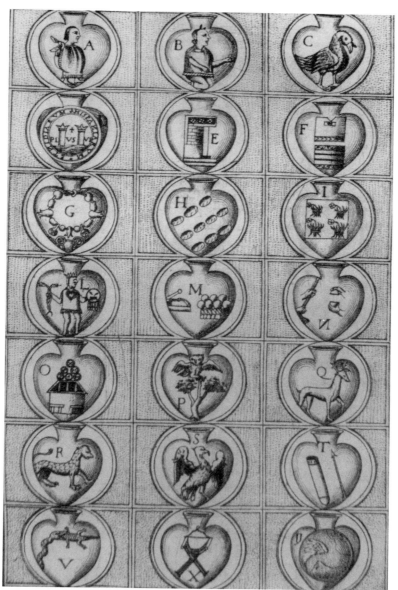

Mnemonic alphabet depicting the relationship between letters and sounds. Sounds are represented by names of individuals and objects. Thus, *A* corresponds to *Antonio,* and so on.

Temple and pyramid surrounded by scenes of Mexica life

Atrio or open air church and related activities. Pedro de Gante can be seen teaching at the upper left (P). At middle right native youths are being taught to write (L).

Friar converting the natives with the assistance of Indian youths
(*behind* the friar)

Friar instructing the natives

Moreover, much of Valadés's account is rhetorical in nature; that is, he focuses on the conversion of the Indians and the methods used by the Franciscans to achieve this conversion. It is, therefore, necessary to consider his account of the indigenous culture before turning to Valadés's theory of rhetoric.

The Civilizing Influence of Rhetoric

One of the principal purposes of the *Rhetorica Christiana* was to provide a testament to the triumphs of the Franciscan missionary endeavors among the other. In his preface Valadés promises to provide

> examples of the successes of the Indies, among whose inhabitants we not only lived, but we were also in charge of them; we believe that this not only served their enjoyment but that it was also beneficial, for ultimately they clearly appreciated the principles, the development, and the practical application of rhetoric, as Cicero attested when he said "There existed a time when men, in the manner of beasts, roamed the earth and struggled for life, and they had neither justice nor virtue of reason but only force. None were legitimate nor knew with certainty who were his children. Then, an excellent man, impelled by some higher motive to unite the men dispersed across the plains and hiding in the woods, converted the fiery savages into peaceful and gentle men." I say that the admirable effects of this influence are nowhere more clearly apparent than in the pacification of the Indians of the New World of the ocean sea.[14]

The role of rhetoric in the New World had been seemingly preordained by Cicero: to bring civilization to human beings who lived like beasts. Whereas Sahagún had invoked the oratorical prowess of the Mexica as a sign of a civilized people, Valadés discerns an absence of rhetorical education which must be rectified before they can be either civilized or Christian. Mesoamerica becomes the site of a grand experiment to confirm the mythic version of civilization's origins found in *De inventione*. This passage, so frequently invoked by Renaissance authors to justify rhetoric's value, now becomes the rationale for expanding the domain of rhetoric to the Americas. More important, Valadés invokes Cicero in the endeavor to legitimize European intervention in the affairs of the natives of the New World.

The purpose of the *Rhetorica Christiana* is therefore twofold: to present general principles of Christian oratory and to record the particular preaching of the Franciscans in Mexico. For Valadés, Cicero's affirmation of rhetoric's civilizing power is more than a commonplace; it is a justification of Franciscan practice and a reflection of Valadés's own experience. That experience was gained by twenty years of preaching among the natives of the New World, a career that gave Valadés a very real appreciation of the power of the spoken word. Valadés attributes much of the success of the Franciscans to their mastery of native languages. Himself accomplished in Nahuatl, Otomi, and Tarascan, he recalls that once the Franciscans had learned the native languages they then proceeded to teach the inhabitants of New Spain "to speak correctly, to write, and to sing."[15] As linguistically adept as many of the Franciscans undoubtedly were, Valadés recognizes that the power of words is not without limits. Not all friars mastered the native languages, and some even persisted in preaching in Latin to Indians untrained in that language. Moreover, explaining Christian theology and Catholic hierarchy to the Mexica proved especially elusive.

Because of the difficulties inherent in attempting to communicate across great cultural barriers, Valadés extols the advantages, indeed the necessity, of augmenting verbal with visual communication. In doing so, Valadés is endorsing what was apparently a common Franciscan practice. The Franciscans resorted to the extensive use of illustrations to supplement sermonizing and to assist teaching. According to Valadés, his order was the first to employ such visual methods in educational endeavors. He therefore felt compelled to include several of these illustrations in the *Rhetorica Christiana* as examples of the Franciscan's pedagogical methods.[16] The preachers made use of large illustrated screens (*lienzos*, literally "linens") as a backdrop to their sermons, allowing the speaker to point to the particular concept or event under discussion. The best-known illustration in the *Rhetorica Christiana* portrays a preacher addressing the Indians and pointing to a series of screens depicting the Passion of Christ.[17] Valadés reports that various aspects of Christian doctrine, including the lives of the apostles, the Decalogue, and the seven deadly sins were demonstrated in this manner.[18] Valadés also includes in the *Rhetorica Christiana* illustrations that were used to graphically represent ecclesiastical and civil themes in addition to theological issues. He presents, for example, elaborately stylized "trees," or organizational charts, designed to show Catholic and Spanish hierarchies to their native "charges." In each case the pope or emperor is at the top of the chart, lesser luminaries occupy the lower branches, and the Indians are at the bottom.[19]

A similar visual method was used to teach the Roman alphabet to the Mexica, an oral people with a pictographic writing system. Valadés presents an elaborate two-page chart in which letters of the alphabet are portrayed with physical objects in order to facilitate the natives' retention of these unfamiliar symbols. These representations are often rather arbitrary and stylized but no more so than the letters with which they are equated. The letter *A*, for example, is represented by a compass and a ladder; *B* is represented by a mandolin; *C* is represented by a horseshoe and a horn; and so on for the entire alphabet. Valadés says that vivid and familiar images ensure that the letters will be remembered. He also presents an alternate system that, although illustrated in a similar manner, is based on sounds rather than shapes. Thus, *A* is equated with the face of a man named Antonio, *B* with Bartolomé, and so on. By such methods Valadés and his Franciscan colleagues undertook to teach a phonetic alphabet to a people to whom such a symbol system was very foreign.[20] For Valadés the use of pictorial representations proved to be a "graceful and fruitful" way to present the word of God to an indigenous audience.[21]

Visual communication is a "fruitful" method, in Valadés's estimation, not simply because the Latin alphabet was alien to the Mexica but also because these people were by nature and by tradition receptive to ideas conveyed by images. Valadés's evidence for this is to be found in the elaborate paintings that the Mexica and other peoples employed as a means of communication.[22] While the Mexica were a predominantly oral culture, they did possess "books" that corresponded closely to the European meaning of the term. While very few of these preconquest codices remain, prior to the Spanish arrival books were sufficiently numerous among the Mexica to require libraries (*amoxcalli*). These books were made of paper derived from the *amate* tree and other materials and folded together rather like a fan or map. The Mexica also recorded information on larger sheets made of cotton and other fibers very similar to the Franciscans' *lienzos*. These books and screens were "written" in the complex glyphs of the Mexica symbol system, which combined numerical, calendrical, pictographic, ideographic, and phonetic glyphs in a very versatile system.[23] With this combination of glyphs the Mexica could record a great deal of information. Says León-Portilla: "It is clear that the Nahuas could write in an unequivocal manner the date, in precise years and days, of any event. Furthermore, with their phonetic system of representation, they could point out the place where each event occurred as well as the names of those who participated in it. They also indicated pictographically numerous details about the event whose record was being committed to paper. Last they were capable of reducing abstract concepts about their religious doctrines, myths and legal ordinances to symbols with their ideographic writing."[24] This system, although highly developed, was not without certain deficiencies. León-Portilla continues: "Those schematic pictures—calendrical-astronomical, doctrinal, or historical—frequently required further explanation. It was not easy (and often impossible) for the Nahuas to indicate in writing the causes of an event, the moral features of a person, or, the countless nuances and modalities that are necessary to narrate or understand fully the doctrines, events, and varieties of human acts and motivations."[25] It was thus necessary to complement this written record with the oral traditions of the Mexica.

Young men, particularly those intended for the priesthood, in the process of learning "good discourse" in the *calmecac*, would therefore be taught to comprehend and explicate the books. In the *General History* Sahagún says of these students: "carefully were they taught the songs which they called the gods' songs. They were inscribed in the books. And well were all taught the reckoning of the days, the book of dreams, and the book of years."[26] This knowledge of books was extremely important in maintaining the traditions of the Mexica. In the *Libro de coloquios* (*Book of Colloquies*) (1524) an anonymous Mexica explained to the first Franciscans the importance of those who kept the books:

> There are those who guide us . . .
> The priests, those who make the offerings . . . ,
> The *tlahtomatinimeh*, sages of the word . . .
> who contemplate,
> follow the content of the books,
> noisily turn their pages, who possess
> the red, the black inks,
> who keep with them the paintings. . . .
> They carry us, guide us,
> those who keep the order of the years
> and know how the days and destinies
> follow their own way.[27]

As this passage suggests, those trained to do so did not literally "read" these texts but did "follow the content of the books." The sequence of pictures and glyphs revealed a complex narrative of traditional events and beliefs. The oral tradition of the Mexica, preserved in their songs, poems, and *huehhuehtlatolli*, was actually the product of a combination of verbal and visual elements. Thus, Valadés's approach of combining sermons with pictures corresponded with the Mexica respect for paintings and their acceptance that illustrations could be the keys to important concepts.

Valadés believed that the Franciscans' campaign of Christianization was successful and that their success was in large measure attributable to the use of methods congenial to the native mind. For Valadés the efficacy of the Franciscans' methods was apparent in the sincerity of those converted to Christianity by the friars. He vigorously and indignantly challenged the charge that the conversion of these new Christians was insincere and that their apparent learning was merely imitation of their masters, much like monkeys.[28] Valadés's argued that the conversion of the Indians of the New World was far more successful than the coercive conversion of the Spanish Muslims of the previous century. This was so because, in the first place, the Indians' conversion to Christianity was done with great care, by ministers using the natives' own tongues. Moreover, according to Valadés, the Indians were by nature more tractable than the Moors.[29] While Valadés admitted that the Indians were not saints, he argued that they were serious about their Christian responsibilities, including communion and confession.[30] Valadés's text leaves little doubt that he regarded the Franciscans' missionary efforts as largely successful. These achievements were due to the sacrifices of the Franciscans, their methods of preaching and teaching, and, of course, divine assistance.

In addition to his accounts of the proselytizing and educational aspects of the Franciscan experience in the New World, Valadés included accounts of the Indians' deities and religious practices. Although the *Rhetorica Christiana* offers fewer details of native life than other works that are strictly chronicles, Valadés nevertheless provides some important information, much of it in the form of illustrations, which is unavailable from other sources. Nevertheless, the *Rhetorica Christiana* is of less importance as a chronicle of the Indies than better-known works such as Sahagún's *General History of the Things of New Spain*. This does not diminish the significance of the *Rhetorica Christiana*, because it is not intended as a comprehensive chronicle of sixteenth-century Mexico but is, rather, a book about rhetoric. And it is rhetoric that occupies the central position in the *Rhetorica Christiana*.

A Rhetoric of Imagery and Memory

The *Rhetorica Christiana* has long been recognized as an important source of information about the Spanish experience in the New World and as an invaluable pictorial account of the great conversion. Yet the work is above all a rhetoric; Valadés's primary goal is to address the needs of the Christian speaker, not only in New Spain but wherever preaching is required. As a work of rhetoric, the *Rhetorica Christiana* is indebted to the standard classical and Renaissance authorities. But, even without Valadés's accounts of indigenous customs and his handsome engravings, the *Rhetorica Christiana* would be a distinctive rhetorical treatise. For, while Valadés's work is comprehensive and often conventional, it nevertheless departs in significant ways from the mainstream of Renaissance rhetoric.

What distinguishes Valadés from other Renaissance rhetoricians, in addition to his account of New World customs, is the importance of memory in his theory of rhetoric. Valadés regards memory as the most important of the five traditional parts of rhetoric. The work was written in Italy at a time of great interest in memory on the peninsula. But the tendency in the late sixteenth century was to exclude memory from rhetoric. Indeed, the large number of Renaissance memory treatises may be a result of the independence of memory from its traditional association with rhetoric. Certainly, the tendency among rhetorical theorists was to deny that memory was a constituent part of rhetoric. Juan Luis Vives, for example, in "De corrupta rhetorica," a part of his encyclopedic *De disciplinis* (1531), explicitly divorces memory from rhetoric, claiming that memory, as a part of nature, belongs equally to all the arts.[31] Granada's *Ecclesiasticae rhetoricae* includes a reference to memory as one of the five parts of rhetoric but omits any extended treatment of memory.

Valadés, by making *memoria* central to the *Rhetorica Christiana*, departs not only from the norms of sixteenth-century rhetoric but also from those of classical rhetorical theory. He does so primarily because memory is essential to the creation of the Christian orator. Valadés's educational program requires mastery of all seven liberal arts in order for the preacher to acquire the encyclopedic knowledge necessary for effective ministry. In advocating such a regimen, Valadés probably had in mind some of the early Franciscans such as Pedro de Gante and Martín de Valencia, who combined courage and piety with great erudition. The variety and depth of learning needed to be a capable Christian orator requires a prodigious memory because memory is "the treasury of the sciences."[32]

In his preface Valadés promises that he will "demonstrate the art of memory cultivation, so long desired by all men." Thus, before any of the other traditional five parts of rhetoric are introduced, Valadés elevates memory to a privileged position, a position it will occupy throughout the treatise. Valadés describes memory as "a firm perception of the soul, of words, and of things, and their placement."[33] Memory, then, is an intellectual process that transcends simple recollection. As such, it is "exceedingly necessary for the orator, is the treasury of invention, and the custodian of all the parts of rhetoric."[34] In Valadés's plan memory does not simply precede invention; it assumes many of the functions more typically assigned to invention.

There are, says Valadés, two types of memory, natural and artificial. Natural memory is a gift of God and is not susceptible to human improvement. Artificial memory, however, which is Valadés's concern, is available to virtually all human beings and may be improved by theory and practice. Valadés's conception of artificial memory is almost entirely visual. It consists, he says, of places and images.[35] Memory, then, is the creation of a "place," an imaginary room, chamber, or, as Valadés suggests, temple, in the mind of the speaker. This place is then filled with vivid images. The speaker then "travels" through this space, encountering images, which prompt the appropriate portion of the speech.

Valadés's conception of artificial memory is derived almost entirely from the Roman treatise of uncertain authorship, the *Rhetorica ad Herennium*.[36] As the only surviving ancient treatise containing a detailed treatment of a classical memory system, the *Ad Herennium* exercised a critical influence on the memory treatises of the Renaissance.[37] Valadés believes the ancient system derived its effectiveness from the virtually universal power of visual imagery. Although this system was first codified by the ancients, Valadés contends that the natives of the New World employ a similar approach to recollection. It is the Indians' aptitude for images which makes artificial memory function for them as surely as it did for the ancient Romans.

Valadés's elevation of memory to the primary position among the traditional five parts of rhetoric naturally had significant consequences on the remaining four. In particular, memory assumes virtually all of the functions typically assigned to invention. Memory is the beginning point of the oration, at which all materials are held and drawn out into discourse. Given this function of memory, invention is necessarily truncated. Valadés does devote part 5 of the *Rhetorica Christiana* to invention, but this is the shortest of the six parts of the work. More significantly, Valadés's discussion of invention really has little similarity to the standard account of argument, topoi, *stasis,* and all the usual apparatus of classical *inventio.* Instead, invention becomes synonymous with the structure of discourse. Although the terminology Valadés employs is that of *dispositio,* he claims that such matters belong to invention: "invention comprises the six parts of the discourse, they are: exordium, narration, digression, division, confirmation, and conclusion."[38] Invention, as the discovery of arguments, is thus replaced by invention as the management of discourse.

Despite removing arguments from the inventional process, Valadés does ultimately discuss argumentation at some length. Arguments, seemingly banished from invention, return in the guise of *elocutio.* Although Valadés had promised in the preface to treat elocution as briefly as possible, he ultimately devotes more attention to it than to any other part of rhetoric, including memory.[39] He begins with a discussion of the figures, which, he says, are "like the clothing and the ornament of discourse."[40] The discussion of figures is followed, not surprisingly, by the discussion of tropes, "the efficacious modification of a word or discourse so that its proper signification is altered."[41]

After this rather traditional discussion of figures and tropes Valadés turns to schemes, which he distinguishes from both tropes and figures. Schemes, says Valadés, "are certain figures and modes of speaking rhetorically. If they are used to illuminate sentences, they are rhetorical ornaments, but if they are formed in order to prove, they pass into the denomination of argumentation or reasoning."[42] These schemes include ratiocination, syllogism, induction, and enumeration. Thus, Valadés recognizes what had been implicit in classical rhetoric: a relationship between style and invention so intimate that argument and ornament sometimes become nearly interchangeable.

After discussing devices that have both an argumentative and a stylistic function, Valadés turns to what he calls simply "arguments." By arguments Valadés means *stasis:* the issues of conjecture, constitution, and quality. The consideration of issues is followed by an enumeration of the places, or topics, of argument. In his treatment of arguments and topoi Valadés is no longer concerned with the stylistic dimension but has returned to the typical argumentative approach he had seemingly abandoned earlier. Argumentation thus remains important to Valadés, but it no longer has a function early in the process of constructing discourse. Instead, the early stages in the creation of discourse are assigned by Valadés to memory. Invention, occurring later in the compositional process, operates much like elocution: it is more a matter of embellishing discourse than creating it. Thus, Valadés treats the standard elements of rhetoric, but he often does so in an unconventional manner. Memory, usually one of the last of the parts of rhetoric to be invoked, becomes the first, and invention, at least in name, becomes disposition, and argument becomes a subspecies of the figures.

The unusual division and recombination of the traditional parts of rhetoric and the intermittent narrative of indigenous culture combine to give the *Rhetorica Christiana* a rather disjointed quality. Although the structure of the treatise is often confusing, there is, nevertheless, a certain unity to it which may not be initially apparent. Indeed, the aspects of the *Rhetorica Christiana* which make it distinctive are also those same features that provide it a certain coherence. Valadés's theory of rhetoric is guided by a belief in the primacy of memory in human discourse. Valadés's conception of memory is, in turn, founded upon a view of the mind which makes mental images central to mental retention and linguistic expression. The emphasis on visualization and mental imagery also provides a psychological foundation for the conversion, both pictorial and verbal, of the Indians. Valadés does not, however, recommend an imagistic approach solely for the Mexica. Rather, the ability of the Indians to apprehend visual images underscores the universality of the appeal of those images. This visual orientation prompted Valadés to illustrate his treatise, in order to render his treatise more appealing and memorable to his readers. Thus, the very elements that separate the *Rhetorica Christiana* from other Renaissance rhetorics are the very aspects that unify Valadés's book.

All of the elements that make up the *Rhetorica Christiana* reflect the conventions of European humanism, but the European antecedents of the work are affected in important ways by Valadés's life in the New World. This is almost certainly the case with regard to the place of memory in the *Rhetorica Christiana*. In an age when many theorists excluded memory from rhetoric, Valadés makes memory more central to rhetoric than ever before. Valadés's elevation of memory was surely a result of his experience among the Mexica, a people for whom the cultivation of memory was inseparable from their symbol system.

The visual elements of the *Rhetorica Christiana* are not, however, solely derived from his New World experience. Valadés's artistry conforms to Renaissance conventions and reflects the influence of European models, especially Albrecht Dürer.[43] Even the Indians in his engravings have a highly Romanized appearance. And certainly rhetoricians had long extolled the virtues of imagery that could make the audience "see" what the speaker was describing. Before Valadés's *Rhetorica Christiana*, however, illustrations had rarely, if ever, been so integral to a work on rhetoric. This is no doubt in part because of Valadés's exceptional artistic ability. But it was also because his New World experience had convinced him that actual images must be joined with mental images for persuasion to be more effective. Again, among the Indians the screens used by the Franciscans were more than clever devices; they were essential to the rhetorical process. They worked where words alone could not.

So, too, the accounts of the Mexica and Chichimecas are not so anomalous as they at first appear. While much of Valadés's rather lengthy account of indigenous customs may not be directly relevant to rhetorical theory, a considerable portion of that account of life in Mexico does illustrate or reinforce Valadés's conception of rhetoric. It is perhaps not simply faulty organization that causes Valadés to insert much of his treatment of the Indians in part 4, otherwise dedicated to the three genera of oratory. Valadés's account of native life follows immediately after his treatment of demonstrative oratory. The placement is probably intentional, because these chapters constitute a lengthy encomium on the virtues of the Indians' character. The account of the Indians is, therefore, not simply informative but is also an example of the principles of demonstrative oratory which preceded it. Valadés intersperses his accounts of the Indians among rhetorical subjects not because of organizational ineptitude but because the life of the natives is truly inseparable from his conception of how rhetoric operates.

It is most improbable that the *Rhetorica Christiana* could have been written the way it was without the long years Valadés spent in New Spain. There is, of course, nothing particularly unique about the treatment of many of the individual subjects included in the *Rhetorica Christiana*. The sixteenth century saw the printing of many preaching manuals, memory treatises, and chronicles of the Indies. But there is almost certainly no other Renaissance treatise that more effectively combines all of these elements into a coherent whole than does the *Rhetorica Christiana*. Valadés stresses the elements he does because of his more than twenty years of preaching among the Indians of Mexico. While Valadés thought of himself as a European and, therefore, a missionary among the Indians, he could not entirely escape his remarkable dual heritage. In the *Rhetorica Christiana* the ancient art of rhetoric confronts, for the first time, the cultural conditions of the New World.

Notes

1. *Rhetorica Christiana: ad concionandi et orandi vsvm accommodata, vtrivsq facvltatis exemplis svo loco insertis; qvae qvidem ex Indorum maxime deprompta svnt historiis. Vnde praeter doctrinam, svma qvoqve . . . delectatio comparabitvr* (Perugia, 1579). I have used the Spanish-Latin edition: *Retórica cristiana*, intro. Esteban J. Palomera, trans. Tarsicio Herrera Zapién et al. (Mexico City: Universidad Nacional Autónoma de México; Fondo de Cultura Económica, 1989). This edition includes reproductions of the original Latin text with the Spanish translation on facing pages. All citations to the *Rhetorica Christiana* are to the original pagination of the Latin text.

2. Ibid., 222.

3. Robert Ricard, *The Spiritual Conquest of Mexico: An Essay on the Apostolate and the Evangelizing Methods of the Mendicant Orders of New Spain, 1523–1572*, trans. Lesley Bird Simpson (Berkeley: University of California Press, 1966), 230.

4. Ibid., 235.

5. *Life in the Imperial and Loyal City of Mexico in New Spain*, trans. Minnie Lee Barrett Shepard (Austin: University of Texas Press, 1953), 7.

6. Francis Borgia Steck, O.F.M., *El primer colegio de América: Santa Cruz de Tlalteloco* (Mexico City: Centro de Estudios Franciscanos, 1944), 34–35; and Pious J. Barth, *Franciscan Education and the Social Order in Spanish North America (1502–1921)* (Ph.D. diss., University of Chicago, 1945), 243–44.

7. *Life in the Imperial and Loyal City of Mexico*, 62.

8. Cited in ibid., 62n.99.

9. Ricard, *Spiritual Conquest*, 223–24.

10. *Rhetorica Christiana*, 184.

11. Ibid., 51. Valadés is, of course, appropriating Quintilian's definition of the orator. For a comparison of Valadés's *Rhetorica Christiana* and Granada's *Ecclesiasticae rhetoricae*, see Palomera, "Introducción," *Retórica cristiana*, xxi–xl.

12. These engravings are discussed by Francisco de la Maza, "Fray Diego Valadés, escritor y grabador franciscano del siglo XVI," *Anales del Instituto de Investigaciones Estéticas* 3 (1945): 15–44. See esp. 35–41.

13. *Rhetorica Christiana*, preface.

14. Ibid.

15. Ibid., 184, 226.

16. Ibid., 95.

17. An obvious copy of this engraving was used by Juan de Torquemada as the frontispiece of his *Monarchia indiana* (1615). More recently Valadés's preacher appears as the jacket illustration of *Renaissance Eloquence*, ed. James J. Murphy (Berkeley: University of California Press, 1983).

18. *Rhetorica Christiana*, 95.

19. Ibid., 180ff.

20. Ibid., 100–101. Alphabets like those presented by Valadés appear in several Renaissance memory treatises, including Jacobus Publicius' *Oratoriae artis epitome* (Venice, 1482), Johannes Romberch's *Congestorium artificiose memoria* (Venice, 1520), and Lodovico Dolce's *Dialogo nel quale si ragiona del modo di accrescere et conservar la memoria* (Venice, 1521). See Francis Yates, *The Art of Memory* (Chicago: University of Chicago Press, 1966), esp. chap. 5, "The Memory Treatises," 105–28. Maza contends that Valadés's alphabet is a copy from Dolce's *Dialogo* ("Fray Diego Valadés, escritor y grabador," 39). While Valadés and the Franciscans did not originate these relatively common Renaissance memory devices, they did adapt them to the teaching of alphabetic literacy in the New World.

21. *Rhetorica Christiana*, 94–96.

22. Ibid., 94.

23. Miguel León-Portilla, *Aztec Image of Self and Society*, ed. Jorge Klor de Alva (Salt Lake City: University of Utah Press, 1992), 44–45.

24. Ibid., 69–70.

25. Ibid., 70.

26. *Florentine Codex*, 4:65.

27. Cited in Miguel León-Portilla, "Have We Really Translated the Mesoamerican 'Ancient Word'?" in *On the Translation of Native American Literatures*, ed. Brian Swann (Washington, D.C.: Smithsonian Institution Press, 1992), 317.

28. *Rhetorica Christiana*, 186.

29. Ibid., 185.

30. Ibid., 184, 188.

31. Juan Luis Vives, *Obras completas*, trans. Lorenzo Riber (Madrid: Aguilar, 1944–48), 2:459.

32. *Rhetorica Christiana*, pt. 3, chap. 24.

33. Ibid., 97.

34. Ibid.

35. Ibid., 89.

36. *Ad C. Herennium*, trans. Harry Caplan (Cambridge: Harvard University Press, 1954), 3:28–40.

37. For a discussion of memory in the *Ad Herennium* and its influence in the Renaissance, see Yates, *Art of Memory*, 1–49.

38. *Rhetorica Christiana*, 228.

39. Ibid., 249–75.

40. Ibid., 249.

41. Ibid., 272.

42. Ibid., 278.

43. For a discussion of Dürer's influence on Valadés, see Maza, "Fray Diego Valadés, escritor y grabador," esp. 36–39.

Chapter 4

Bartolomé de Las Casas and José de Acosta
The Other as Audience

An essential aspect of rhetoric is, in the words of Kenneth Burke, "its nature as *addressed,* since persuasion implies an audience."[1] The existence of an audience, in turn, requires that the rhetor possess some knowledge of the beings to be addressed. Early in the history of classical rhetoric theorists began to grapple with the problem of how the speaker might understand and accommodate an audience. Thus, in Plato's *Phaedrus* Socrates says that, "since it is the function of speech to lead souls by persuasion, he who is to be a rhetorician must know the various forms of the soul."[2] Therefore, the speaker "must understand the nature of the soul, must find out the class of speech adapted to each nature, and must arrange and adorn his discourse accordingly, offering to the complex soul elaborate and harmonious discourses, and simple talks to the simple soul."[3]

Plato's admonitions to know the soul apparently prompted Aristotle to investigate the psyche of the orator's audience. This investigation culminated in the famous account of the emotions in book 2 of his *Rhetoric.* These chapters, "the earliest systematic discussion of human psychology," would long remain one of the most complete expositions of the emotional states of the audience.[4] The obligation of the rhetor to engage the audience emotionally is further developed by Cicero in *De Oratore.* In this dialogue the character Antonius says that "the whole art of speaking rests on three things to bring about persuasion, that we prove what we allege to be true, that we win the favor of the audience, that we arouse in their minds whatever feelings our case may require."[5] This leads to Cicero's dictum that there are "three things which alone have the power to persuade: that the minds of the hearers be won over, instructed, and moved."[6] Cicero's three "duties" of the orator—to instruct, to win, and to move the audience—were endorsed by Augustine and thus became a part of Christian rhetoric. Christian rhetoricians did not merely accept the necessity of emotional appeal, but strongly embraced the place of the passions in persuasion. As a result of Augustinian psychology, says Debora Shuger, volition and affect become inseparable, and "passionate oratory, oratory that moves the emotions and loves of the soul, becomes a powerful instrument of redemption. The grand style dominates Renaissance sacred rhetorics because it alone can transform the will and the heart, turning them toward love of God and neighbor."[7]

Classical and Renaissance rhetoricians were greatly concerned about the human passions and how those passions might be invoked to produce persuasion. And, while these rhetoricians attended to the variety of human emotional states, they were relatively uninterested in the differences among human beings. The audience implicit in virtually all theories was more or less a reflection of the theorist. The imagined audience might differ from the speaker, in age or wealth or mental acuity, but the variations were rather slight. Renaissance rhetoricians were content to assume, with little discussion, a fundamental identification between rhetor and auditor.

Rhetoricians rarely addressed the issue of audiences culturally and ethnically distinct from the speaker because there was little incentive for them to do so. It was not until the explorations of the late fifteenth century that communication with non-Europeans appeared to deserve serious consideration.[8] Then in the following century, when the conquests of Cortés and Pizarro created a multitude of potential Christian converts, the need to consider the means of addressing audiences radically different from European congregations became imperative. These newly acquired colonial subjects were curious peoples with peculiar customs and a disconcerting disinterest in the Gospel. This American audience presented the Christian orator with perplexing problems about which classical rhetoric offered little insight. Missionaries addressing indigenous audiences would need to reconcile traditional theory with colonial exigencies or devise new rhetorical strategies for addressing the other.

The problems presented by the newly encountered audience are addressed by two of the most important missionaries to the New World: Bartolomé de Las Casas and José de Acosta. Both men labored long and hard in the New World, both wrote histories of the "Indies," and both wrote about the nature of the peoples of the Americas and how to preach to them.

The One Method of Bartolomé de Las Casas

Bartolomé de Las Casas devoted most of his long life to preaching, writing, and debating on behalf of the natives of the New World. As a result, he is one of the best known and widely studied of all the clerics involved in the enterprise of the Indies. Las Casas, born in 1474, went to the island of Hispaniola as a settler in 1502. While on Hispaniola he was admitted to the priesthood. In 1512 he participated in the conquest of Cuba. His reward for this participation was an *encomienda,* a trusteeship over the native population in a specified area. The *encomienda* was, in effect, a form of slavery, which became of one the most notorious institutions in the Spanish colonies. Not long after becoming an *encomendero,* Las Casas, prompted by the preaching of the Dominicans, began to have serious doubts about the system he would do much to make infamous. In 1514 he renounced his *encomienda* and preached his first sermon against the system. From then on he devoted himself to securing a more humane policy toward the native peoples of Spain's American empire. His opposition to the *encomienda* was so outspoken and strident that in 1516 he was designated the "official protector" of the Indians on Hispaniola. In 1543 Las Casas was elected bishop of Chiapas.

In 1550 and 1551 Las Casas was a protagonist in a remarkable debate on the nature of the peoples of the New World before a council summoned by Charles V at Valladolid. Las Casas's opponent, the humanist Juan Ginés de Sepúlveda, advanced a theory of the Indian's innate inferiority, thereby justifying warfare and enslavement to ensure their conversion to Christianity.[9] The debate was long, and, because the assembled theologians never rendered a final verdict, the results were inconclusive. After the debate at Valladolid, Las Casas remained in Spain, finishing his *Historia de las Indias* and securing the printing of many of several works completed earlier. He died in Madrid in 1566.

Las Casas's views on the nature of the Indians are most fully presented in his *Historia de las Indias* and his *Apologética historia (In Defense of the Indians).* His approach to preaching and conversion is developed in *De unico vocationis modo omnium gentium ad veram religionem (The Only Way to Attract All People to the True Religion).*[10] *De unico vocationis modo* was Las Casas's first major work, which he had completed by 1540, perhaps even earlier.[11] Regrettably, there are only three extant chapters of what must have been a very long book; the surviving chapters consist of nearly three hundred pages of Latin text. Fortunately, however, Antonio de Remesal includes a brief synopsis of the entire work in his *Historia general de las Indias Occidentales y particular de la gobernación de Chiapa y Guatemala* (1619).[12] Las Casas's three extant chapters, together with his other writings and Remesal's summary, provide a reasonably complete view of his theory of evangelization.

De unico vocationis modo is a detailed elaboration of its title: there is only one method of converting people to Christianity, that method is peaceful persuasion, and it is a method that applies to all peoples of the world. Like virtually all of Las Casas's writings, *De unico vocationis modo* is closely argued, thoroughly documented with biblical, ecclesiastical, and classical references, and remarkably repetitive. It is also clear and unambiguous. Las Casas is emphatic that there can be no exceptions to the requirement of persuasion by peaceful means. Much of this work, therefore, like his better-known writings, is an indictment of the doctrine of a "just war" against the Indians as a legitimate means to secure conversion.

Las Casas's fundamental proposition is advanced early in chapter 5 (the first of the extant chapters): "Divine providence has established, for all the world and for all times, one and only one method which teaches men the true religion, that which persuades the understanding by reason and invention and gently attracts the will. Indubitably, this method must be common to all men of the world, without distinction because of sects, errors, or corruption of customs."[13] According to Remesal, Las Casas begins his case in support of this proposition by arguing the essential uniformity of all human beings. First, Las Casas argues that Christ, in affirming the predestination of all peoples of the earth, excluded no nation from this promise, and therefore the New World of the Indies is necessarily included.[14] Because all are predestined for salvation, all must necessarily possess the intelligence required to comprehend the message of salvation. Therefore, it is "not possible that there is an entire nation, people, city, or town that is so without understanding as to be incapable of accepting the gospel."[15] While the natives of the Indies, like all peoples, varied in their intellectual capacity, they must be included among those possessed of common sense, imagination, memory, and judgment.[16]

Because the Amerindians were reasoning beings, they could be, indeed they must be, persuaded to accept Christianity in a way that was peaceful and rational. For Las Casas there was simply no other method of evangelization that could be justified, either morally or practically.

He demonstrates the superiority of his "one method" through an accumulation of historical and theological evidence. Las Casas identifies this one method of peaceful persuasion as the method of classical rhetoric. The preacher who has been entrusted, says Las Casas, "to instruct and attract men to the faith and true religion must study the nature and principles of rhetoric, and must diligently observe its precepts in preaching, in order to move and attract the soul of the audience."[17] The successful preacher must fulfill the requirements of the orator stipulated by Cicero in *De oratore:* "for the purposes of persuasion the art of speaking relies wholly on three things: the proof of our allegations, the winning of our hearers' favors and the rousing of their feelings to whatever impulse our case may require."[18]

Las Casas also reminds his readers that it was rhetoric, rather than force, which forged human civilization. His evidence, of course, is the familiar passage from *De inventione* (which he quotes at length) proclaiming the civilizing properties of rhetoric.[19] For Las Casas this transformational power is the essence of the art of rhetoric. Persuasion, without "the violence of arms, without force against natural reason," can transform beasts into human beings and teach savages "to love justice, equity, and virtue and, ultimately, to revere the faith, that is, to revere God."[20] Las Casas, then, recommends peaceful persuasion because of its role in the creation of European civilization. An even more important precedent for peaceful persuasion, of course, was its role in the ministry of Christ. Because Christ both advocated and practiced peaceful conversion, it was incumbent upon his followers to do likewise. In support of his position Las Casas includes the entire text of the bull *Sublimis Deus* of Pope Paul III (1537). The bull declares that the "Indians, as true men, not only are capable of receiving the Christian faith, but as we have learned, are eager to receive it." Therefore, "the Indians and other nations must be invited to receive the said faith of Christ with the preaching of the word of God and with examples of a good life."[21] Thus, classical tradition, Christian practice, and papal authority all validate peaceful persuasion as the only legitimate method of conversion.

Las Casas concedes that the success of the method, despite the precedents endorsing its use, cannot be guaranteed. Rather, the efficacy of persuasion depends upon the character of the preacher. Las Casas advances five conditions essential for preaching the Gospel effectively. First, hearers, "and most especially infidels," must understand that the preacher does not seek to establish dominance over the addressed.[22] Second, the hearers must further recognize that the preacher does not preach from a desire for wealth.[23] Third, the preacher must speak in a manner "sweet and humble, affable and gentle, kind and benevolent," in order to instill in the hearers a desire to voluntarily attend to and accept Christian doctrine. Fourth, preachers must show the same love and charity toward humanity as did Saint Paul.[24] Fifth, and finally, the preacher must live "an exemplary life, resplendent with virtuous works; a life that offends no one and is totally above reproach."[25] The responsibility for communicating the message of Christianity rests entirely with the preacher. The preacher is obligated, through word and deed, to present the Gospel in a manner that will appeal to the understanding and to the soul. Even if the preacher can fulfill these five requirements, conversion of the audience is not assured. Las Casas recognizes that winning hearts and minds is a slow and uneven process, but for him there can be no alternative.

Las Casas devotes the last of the extant chapters to a condemnation of conversion by force. He argues that, even when peaceful methods appear too slow and too uncertain, force cannot be justified, for it is always contrary to Christian doctrine. The use of force should be rejected by Christians, because it is typical of the false religion of "the pseudoprophet and seductor of men," Mohammed.[26] Not only is the use of force un-Christian; it is also ineffective because it invariably results in resentment and false conversion. The success of forced conversions is illusory and transitory.

Despite the disadvantages of forceful conversion, Las Casas does not reject unconditionally all uses of force. In certain circumstances force may be used against particular classes of infidels. Las Casas categorizes infidels into four classes; each class should be accorded different treatment by Christians. The first class is composed of those infidels who live among Christians, such as the Jews and Moors of Castile, who are subject to Christian laws. The second class of infidels consists of those who oppose Christianity by force and violence, such as the Turks and Moors of Africa; against this class of infidels the use of force is justified and necessary. The third class of infidels encompasses those who have rejected true Christianity, the heretics and apostates of Europe. The fourth and final class of infidels includes those who have never been exposed to Christianity, who have lived apart from the Christian world and thus have never offended the church; it is in this class, of course, that the peoples of the Indies belong. The only appropriate behavior toward this class of infidels is to persuade them to join the Christian faith.[27] To wage war on these infidels is "reckless, unjust, and tyrannical."[28]

In *De unico vocationis modo* Las Casas says almost as much about the inappropriateness of violence as a means of conversion as he says about the appropriateness of peaceful persuasion. This is because *De unico vocationis modo* is an integral part of his campaign in defense of the Indians. In order for Las Casas to establish peaceful persuasion as the exclusive method of conversion requires that he completely discredit the doctrine of just war. Although the surviving chapters of *De unico vocationis modo* constitute a lengthy text, Las Casas's argument is quite simple: the natives of the New World are rational people, and, consequently, they must be persuaded to accept Christianity in a rational manner. No other approach can be tolerated. Beyond affirming their essential rationality, Las Casas says remarkably little about the Indians. Because he believes in the identity of the Indians and all other human beings, Las Casas sees little need to comment on particular customs and practices. Like Europeans, Americans possess intelligence and imagination, and therefore the missionary may employ the traditional methods of classical rhetoric in the New World. Las Casas is content to endorse the utility of traditional rhetorical theory without attempting a significant revision of it for missionary purposes. In this insistence on the necessity of one method for the persuasion of all human beings, he is exceptional. Others, as intent as Las Casas to Christianize the New World, would conclude that the variations of humanity require a multiplicity of methods of conversion.

The Many Methods of José de Acosta

José de Acosta, much like Bartolomé de Las Casas, understood the importance of effective communication to the success of the evangelical enterprise. Also like Las Casas, he recognized the precariousness of such communication. Acosta's speculation and advice on such matters are most fully presented in *De procuranda indorum salute* (*On Procuring the Salvation of the Indians*), but his attention to the rhetorical problems inherent in the Christianization of the Americas appears throughout his writings.

Acosta, born in Spain in 1540, entered the Jesuit order in 1552 and was educated at Jesuit *colegios* and then at the University of Alcalá. In 1567 he became professor of theology at the Jesuit college of Ocaña and in 1571 was transferred to the college of Plasencia. Later the same year he departed for Peru, arriving in Lima in 1572. Acosta was to exercise great influence over the intellectual and religious life of the colony. He became rector of the college of San Pablo in 1575, and the next year he was named the Jesuit provincial of Peru. In 1582 and 1583 he served as the official theologian of the Third Provincial Council of Lima. In 1586 he set off for Europe, visiting Mexico along the way, returning to his native Spain in 1587. Acosta died in Salamanca in 1600.

Not long after his arrival in the New World Acosta recognized the need for a practical manual for the missionary experience. Thus, he began to work on *De procuranda* in 1577 and had probably completed the manuscript by 1578. In about 1581 he began to work on an account of the New World, *De natura novi orbis*. Finally, in 1588, the two works were published together under the title *De natura novi orbis, libro duo, et de promulgatione evangelii, apud barbaros, sive de procuranda indorum salute, libri sex*. Two years later Acosta published his *Historia natural y moral de las Indias*. This work consists of two chapters describing the geographical and ecological characteristics of the New World—essentially a Spanish translation of the two books of *De natura novi orbis*—followed by another five chapters detailing the customs and habits of the inhabitants of the Indies. The original publication of *De procuranda* and *De natura novi orbis* in a single volume clearly indicates that Acosta recognizes that an understanding of the lands and people of the New World is inseparable from the missionary undertaking.

Intervening between the completion of *De procuranda* and its publication was an important ecclesiastical event in which Acosta figured prominently: the Third Provincial Council of Lima (1583). A significant result of the council was the publication in 1585 of the *Tercero catecismo y exposición de la doctrina christiana por sermones* (*Third Catechism and Exposition of Christian Doctrine through Sermons*). This work, intended as a guide to the conversion process, includes a trilingual (Spanish, Quechua, Aymara) catechism and a collection of sermons. Although his name does not appear on the title page, Acosta is the principal author of the Spanish text.[29] In the *"Proemio"* of this work, *"Del modo que se ha de tener en enseñar, y predicar a los Indios"* ("The Method of Teaching and Preaching to the Indians"), Acosta presents a series of instructions for the missionary to follow when converting the Peruvians. Taken together, the *Tercero catecismo* and the *De procuranda* present one of the most complete and influential theories of preaching and conversion produced by the colonial church.

Acosta's first recommendation in the *Tercero catecismo* to the missionary preacher is to always "accommodate the capacity of the audience."[30] While this advice is little more than a repetition of standard rhetorical doctrine, Acosta recognizes that the implementation of his directives presents considerable difficulties. One of the greatest of those difficulties is determining the precise "capacity" of the preacher's audience. Thus, a considerable portion of Acosta's work examines the nature of the natives in order to provide the missionary with the information needed to accommodate the aboriginal audience.

Acosta believes that the problems facing the preacher are compounded by the lack of reliable information available to the missionary. Indeed, Acosta's works are filled with warnings about the great difficulties facing the missionary in the New World. "It is very difficult," he says, "to speak correctly and with certainty about the ministry of the salvation of the Indians."[31] While he does not want to criticize "ignorant experts," Acosta says that there are those who believe that all Indians are the same.[32] Nothing could be either more inaccurate nor more misleading to the potential preacher. Indeed, Acosta maintains that the native peoples are so numerous that he could not possibly discuss them all. He therefore sensibly decides to concentrate on Peru, advising his readers to adapt his recommendations to other situations.[33] Having cautioned his readers that the natives of the New World vary greatly in customs and abilities, Acosta undertakes to classify the various sorts of barbarians who inhabit the earth. Acosta, who is vitally interested in the possibility of communication, selects as his primary criteria for classification a linguistic category: alphabetic literacy. The more closely a barbarian's writing system approximates the Roman alphabet, the greater the possibility becomes of civilizing and Christianizing such peoples. Thus, Acosta presents a tripartite classification of the barbarians living in various parts of the world according to the level of literacy exhibited by each group.

The first and highest group in Acosta's scheme are those peoples who have "stable political regimes, public laws, fortified cities, respected magistrates, prosperous and well-organized commerce, and, most importantly, the understanding and use of letters."[34] Such highly advanced barbarians, claims Acosta, are to be found only in Asia and include the Chinese, the Japanese, and certain inhabitants of the East Indies. The second class of barbarians includes those who, despite their ignorance of the alphabet, have nevertheless been able to achieve a relatively high degree of political, military, and religious organization. In this second class Acosta places "our Mexicans and Peruvians, whose empires, systems of government, laws and institutions the entire world can justly admire."[35] The third and lowest class of barbarians are those "savage men, similar to beasts," who live without the benefit of laws or magistrates or any kind of established civic life. These are the barbarians of *De inventione,* living like beasts in the fields.[36] Although it is impossible to know how many of these barbarians there are, Acosta says there are "innumerable herds" of these primitive people in the New World.[37]

Acosta argues that barbarianism is not so much a natural condition as it is a product of custom and education. Implicit in Acosta's hierarchy is his conviction that barbarians are capable of progressing from the lowest to the highest categories and perhaps even beyond. As proof of this, he notes that Spain itself was once a wild and barbarous place but is now civilized.[38] Acosta adds that even in Spain there are isolated areas, such as Asturias and Cantabria, where uneducated peasants can still resemble barbarians. Like Spain, the New World, too, will eventually be civilized.

Acosta's tripartite classification of barbarians is intended to aid the evangelist in adapting to the New World audience. The possible methods of conversions are directly linked to the classes of barbarians to whom they are to be applied. Thus, just as there are three classes of barbarians, so too are there three methods of evangelization. The first of these methods is that employed by Christ's apostles, who relied on the spoken word, peaceful persuasion without the assistance of military intervention. Like many Europeans, Acosta saw the great evangelistic campaign to convert the New World as the latter-day equivalent of the original apostles' efforts to Christianize the Roman Empire. Acosta would like to replicate the methods, and the successes, of the first apostles but concludes that these earlier apostolic practices are not entirely appropriate to New World conditions. Such techniques were successful among the ancient Greeks and Romans because their intellectual capacity allowed them to fully appreciate the apostle' message. Likewise, in Acosta's day such methods could be effective only among the first class of barbarians, those peoples whose literacy confirmed their status as fully rational beings. Obviously, then, because he found no such people in the New World, Acosta rejects the original, apostolic method of Christian conversion as inapplicable to Spain's American colonies.[39]

The "old methods" of conversion were inappropriate, first and foremost, because of the limited ability of the Indian audience. Acosta also identifies a second reason that such methods could not be used: the absence of miracles in America. Acosta was deeply troubled by the inability of those engaged in Christianizing the New World to be assisted by miraculous events. If the conversion campaign in the New World were the equivalent of the earlier conversion of Europe, present-day evangelists ought to expect the same divine assistance. The reason miracles no longer occur, Acosta decides, is that, despite some similarities between the earliest days of Christianity and his own times, the situation is very different. The difference, once again, rests with the inhabitants of the New World. "Those to whom we proclaim the faith," says Acosta, when compared to the Greeks and Romans, "are completely inferior: in intellect, in culture, and in ability."[40] Such an audience would be incapable of understanding the significance of miracles, thus rendering them useless.

Acosta concludes his discussion of miracles by asking: "What necessity is there of great miracles when what is lacking is a sufficient intelligence to perceive the curiosity to understand the profundity of our doctrine? Only one singular and unique miracle is necessary. A miracle most important for the people of the New World and most efficacious for the propagation of the faith, that is that the customs of the missionary are consistent with his faith. This miracle is more than sufficient."[41] While Acosta recognizes the indiscretions of the missionaries, it is the inferiority of the Indians which prevents the use of miracles as an aid to the missionary endeavor. Thus, the Indians of the New World lack the capacity to appreciate either rational persuasion or divine intervention. And so the methods of the first apostles cannot be used in the New World, although persuasion, at least, may presumably be employed in Asia.

With the original method of evangelization thus eliminated, Acosta proposes strategies he believes appropriate to the barbarians of the New World. The methods appropriate to the third class of barbarians, those lacking any civilization, is a combination of peaceful persuasion and military coercion. Although Acosta is adamantly opposed to a "just war" of extermination against those unwilling to accept Christianity, he is not reluctant to endorse aggressive measures to compel Christianization.[42] Thus, for proselytizing barbarians of the third class he recommends the assistance of soldiers to protect the missionaries and to ensure exposure to the message.

The remaining method of conversion is directed toward those barbarians who, like the Mexica and the Inca, are not fully literate and yet possess highly developed social and political institutions. Acosta suggests that a "Christian prince" be imposed on such peoples and that such a ruler be responsible for maintaining a Christian community.[43] Acosta is quite clear that the traditional methods of the apostles will be ineffective with the second class of barbarians and can thus be discarded by the missionary in the New World. He is much less explicit, however, about the alternatives. His two additional methods of imposing Christian rulers and supplementing preaching with military coercion seems to be little more than an affirmation of Spanish imperial policy. What is needed, if he is going to reject traditional methods, is an alternative that can be used in the missionary endeavor in the New World.

This alternative is at least partially sketched in the *Tercero catecismo*. Acosta first advises that the missionary accommodate the capabilities of the indigenous audience. His three remaining directives help explain how this accommodation might be accomplished. Acosta's second directive to the missionary is to repeat upon "diverse occasions the principal points of Christian Doctrine" so that such points will become fixed in the auditor's memory. In particular, Acosta recommends the constant repetition of "the unity of the one God, the prohibition of worshipping other gods, Jesus as son of God and son of man and savior of human kind."[44] Acosta, frustrated by the Peruvians' persistent adherence to their "superstitions," believes that tenacity of the audience could be overcome by the perseverance of the preacher.[45]

The fundamentals of Christian doctrine require not only constant repetition but simplicity of style as well. Acosta's third recommendation to the missionary, therefore, is that the method of presenting the faith must be "plain, simple, clear, and brief."[46] The speeches to the Indians must be in a style "simple and humble, not elevated; the clauses neither long nor roundabout, the language neither exquisite nor affected; more in the manner of discourse among friends, rather than the declamation of the theater."[47] In advocating a plain and simple style, Acosta is largely rejecting the dominant mode of sacred oratory recommended in rhetorical treatises. As Shuger indicates, "from the late fifteenth to the late seventeenth century, there are dozens of learned and thoughtful rhetorics advocating a passionate and religious lofty prose." These "sacred rhetorics of the Renaissance emphasize the passion, sublimity, and grandeur of sacred discourse, grounding these qualities in the classical grand style and the principles of Renaissance theology and psychology."[48]

Acosta recommends a modification of recognized rhetorical norms because he is convinced that the natives of the New World cannot ap-

preciate the grand style of European oratory. While he recognizes variations in the capacity of the Indians, the Indians are invariably of vastly
lesser capacity than a civilized audience. In *De procuranda* Acosta argues
that the barbarian's incapacity is a result of educational deprivation and
Spanish abuse rather than a natural condition, thus implying that the
Indians can evolve into civilized Christians. He gives little indication,
however, that he has seen much evidence of such progress during his
time in Peru.

Acosta's attribution of the Indians' limitations to educational deprivation often seems disingenuous. Indeed, Acosta at times appears convinced that the Indians are not only inferior to Europeans but also that
such inferiority is a natural condition. In *De procuranda* Acosta says that
the Indians are "servile by nature" and that Indians, like "Ethiopians,"
are no more rational than animals.[49] One indication of this irrationality
is that the Spanish "proclaim the mysteries of the faith and they [the
Indians] do not understand."[50] The proclamations are repeated again
and again, just as Acosta advises, yet they rarely yield the desired result.
He also recommends preaching no more than the basic dogma to the
Peruvians, and yet even that seems beyond the grasp of the audience.
Acosta is troubled by this apparent intransigence on the part of the Indians. If the basic doctrines were beyond the abilities of the indigenous
audience, the entire missionary endeavor must necessarily be jeopardized. Thus, the Spanish missionary establishment sought ways to make
the doctrines of their faith comprehensible to peoples presumed to be of
attenuated aptitude either as a result of nature or custom. A poetic effort
to explain the Trinity to a native audience is presented by the Franciscan
Luís Gerónimo de Oré (1554–1629) in his *Symbolo Catholico Indiano* (1598):

> It is in the Catholic faith that we should venerate one God in
>   Trinity and a Trinity in Unity.
> We must not confuse the persons nor separate the substance.
> Distinct is the person of the Father, distinct is the person of the Son
>   and distinct the person of the Holy Spirit.
> Yet the divinity of the Father, the Son and the Holy Spirit is one,
>   with equal glory and majesty.
> In this the Father and the Son and the Holy Spirit are equal.
> The father is uncreated, the Son is uncreated and the Holy Spirit is
>   uncreated.
> The Father is incomprehensible, the Son is incomprehensible and
>   the Holy Spirit is incomprehensible.[51]

The challenge for the missionary is to make the incomprehensible comprehensible to an audience assumed to be rather simpleminded. This responsibility might suggest that Acosta would favor the catechistic approach of Augustine's *De catechizandis rudibus* for the Amerindian audience, yet the fourth and final recommendation in the *Tercero catecismo* indicates otherwise. Last, and most important, says Acosta, the preacher must present doctrine in a manner that is not only comprehensible but also persuasive.[52] The catechism is appropriate for providing the Indians with an understanding of doctrine but is not necessarily sufficient to compel adherence to that doctrine. This requires "a different style, one that is to be like that of the sermon or speech of the sermon, and one which teaches, pleases, and moves the hearers, so that they receive the doctrine of God and keep it."[53] The preacher in the New World, like any Christian orator, must fulfill the Ciceronian (and Augustinian) three-fold duty to teach, to please, and to move. The responsibility of the missionary is, finally, as much rhetorical as theoretical: the audience must be persuaded. Acosta says that experience has shown that "these Indians (like other men) are usually persuaded more by moving their emotions than by reasoning."[54] Thus, it is "important in the sermons to use those things which provoke and awaken the affections, like apostrophes, exclamations, and other figures taught by the art of oratory."[55] Acosta advocates a plain and simple style of preaching, but he does not favor a style so austere that the captivation of the emotions is jeopardized.

Acosta recognizes that, while a lively style is a prerequisite for emotional engagement, persuasion is not solely a product of the appropriate style. At the end of the *Proemio* of the *Tercero catecismo* Acosta emphasizes that persuasion requires the preacher to be a model of the Christian message, a theme he also develops in *De procuranda*. In that work Acosta, invoking Augustine, whom he calls "the discoverer of sacred oratory," argues that piety is more important than oratory in the salvation of souls.[56] He maintains that "the barbarians do not understand our sermons well, but examples of virtue speak with clarity everywhere, are understood perfectly, and have the maximum power of persuasion."[57] The missionary, therefore, must be "patient, humble, generous, sober, gentle, but above all consumed with the love of Christ."[58] Acosta recognizes, however, that the Spanish colonists often exhibited a less desirable list of traits. Like Las Casas, Acosta is especially critical of the *encomienda* system.[59] Acosta believes that Spaniards behaved with such "avarice, violence, and tyranny" that they "greatly retarded the conversion of the Indians."[60]

Although Acosta laments the behavior of Spanish colonists and even missionaries, he leaves no doubt that the greatest impediments to the spread of Christianity in the New World are the "inveterate customs of the infidels."[61] Acosta admits that all peoples value traditions, but barbarians, because of their limited reason, cling to their customs with greater tenacity than civilized people.[62] Thus, says Acosta, while it is "difficult to train brute animals, it is even harder to dislodge the customs of men of limited intelligence."[63] As difficult as it is "to eradicate natural inclinations and inveterate customs," Acosta remains convinced that such customs will change, "little by little," and for the better.[64]

Acosta frequently reminds his readers that conversion of the natives of the New World is a slow and arduous task made more difficult by the incapacity and irrationality of the potential converts. The missionaries' audience, intellectually limited and spiritually deluded, must be accommodated by a message that is simple and repetitive yet persuasive. Acosta perhaps best summarizes his own method when he offers this advice to missionaries in *De procuranda*: "Captivate with words, stimulate with rewards, frighten with threats, persuade with examples, but trust in the virtue of Christ and not in the knowledge of men."[65]

Both Bartolomé de Las Casas and José de Acosta were dedicated to the "spiritual conquest" of the New World. They also shared a recognition of the missionary's need to engage in direct communication with the native audience in order to achieve conversion. To facilitate communication and conversion Las Casas and Acosta wrote two of the earliest and most complete treatises on the evangelization of the New World. Yet, despite sharing much in common, Las Casas and Acosta differ in fundamental ways. The most basic disagreement between the Dominican and the Jesuit is, of course, their conception of the nature of the inhabitants of America. Las Casas earned his title as the "defender of the Indians" by advocating the essential rationality, the fundamental humanity, of the Americans. Acosta does not share Las Casas's undifferentiated view of humanity. In his hierarchy barbarians are inferior to Europeans, and the barbarians of America are inferior to the barbarians of Asia. When Acosta does defend the humanity of the Indians, he offers an ambivalent defense at best. Often he characterizes them as irrational and intransigent, barely more tractable than wild animals.

Given their very different views of the Indies' inhabitants, it is inevitable that Las Casas and Acosta would construct rather different theories of how the missionary might profitably address the other. Las Casas's approach is quite simple. The Indians, being in all respects human, can be addressed in the traditional ways endorsed by both classical and Christian tradition. There is no reason, therefore, that the precepts of Cicero and Augustine, long useful for Europeans, should not be employed with equal efficacy among Mexicans and Peruvians. Las Casas is confident that the methods of the original apostles could thus be replicated by their successors in the New World. The unfamiliar customs and practices of the audience are far less important than their basic humanity. The audience, therefore, receives little attention from Las Casas. The speaker, on the other hand, assumes great importance. For Las Casas the speaker, as the exemplar of the good Christian, is the centerpiece of sacred oratory.

Acosta's approach to preaching among the other is more complex than that proposed by Las Casas because it is based on discriminations among barbarians. While there are barbarians capable of appreciating complex persuasive appeals, they are not to be found among the inhabitants of the New World. Traditional persuasive methods are therefore mostly irrelevant to the missionary in America. Natives of the New World must be presented with simple, repetitive messages, for they can comprehend nothing more. And, while Acosta rejects the idea of a just war against infidels, he nevertheless endorses force as a useful incentive to conversion. For him the audience overshadows the speaker in the rhetorical situation. Acosta naturally endorses the need for the preacher to be exemplary, but it is ultimately the audience that dictates the strategies the speaker must employ. Thus, the techniques of rhetoric, while always helpful, are of more limited utility to the New World missionary than to the European preacher. The communication is always controlled by the capacity—or, more precisely, the incapacity—of the audience.

De unico vocationis modo and *De procuranda* present very different views about the nature of the audience, the other, and therefore different views about the utility of rhetoric itself in the New World. Las Casas, embracing the American audience as essentially one with all humanity, recommends the use of classical rhetoric with little concern about adapting it to new conditions. Acosta denigrates that same audience and by doing so permits only an abbreviated version of traditional rhetoric to be profitably applied by the missionary. Las Casas and Acosta do agree that the precepts of rhetoric are useful only when the speaker's audience is fully human. Ultimately, therefore, it is the conception of the peoples of the New World which determines the place of rhetoric in it.

Notes

1. *A Rhetoric of Motives* (Berkeley: University of California Press, 1969), 38.
2. Trans. Harold North Fowler (Cambridge: Harvard University Press, 1982), 271D.
3. Ibid., 277B–C.
4. Aristotle, *On Rhetoric: A Theory of Civic Discourse*, trans. George A. Kennedy (New York: Oxford University Press, 1991), 122.
5. Trans. E. W. Sutton and H. Rackham (Cambridge: Harvard University Press, 1976), II.xxvii.114–15.
6. Ibid., II.xxviii.121.
7. *Sacred Rhetoric: The Christian Grand Style in the English Renaissance* (Princeton: Princeton University Press, 1988), 48.
8. For discussions of the effect of the New World on European anthropological conceptions, see Anthony Pagden, *The Fall of Natural Man: The American Indian and the Origins of Comparative Ethnology* (Cambridge: Cambridge University Press, 1982), esp. 1–26; and Lewis Hanke, *Aristotle and the American Indians: A Study in Race Prejudice in the Modern World* (London: Hollis and Carter, 1959), esp 1–27.
9. For accounts of this debate, see Hanke, *Aristotle and the American Indians*, 28–73; and Angel Losada, "The Controversy between Sepúlveda and Las Casas in the Junta of Valladolid," in *Bartolomé de Las Casas in History: Toward an Understanding of the Man and His Work,* ed. Juan Friede and Benjamin Keen (DeKalb: Northern Illinois University Press, 1971), 279–308.
10. For bibliographies of writings by and about Las Casas, see "Narrative and Critical Catalogue of Casas' Writings," in *The Life and Writings of Bartolomé de las Casas,* ed. Henry Wagner and Helen Parish (Albuquerque: University of New Mexico Press, 1967), 251–98; and Raymond Marcus, "Las Casas: A Selective Bibliography," in Friede and Keen, *Bartolomé de Las Casas in History,* 603–16.
11. Wagner dates the completion of this work at 1538–40 (*Life and Writings,* 98). Manual Martínez argues for an earlier date: 1527 ("Las Casas on the Conquest of America," in *Bartolomé de las Casas in History,* 314–15).
12. *Biblioteca de autores españoles,* vol. 175 (Madrid: Atlas, 1964), 209–12.
13. *Del único modo de atraer a todos los pueblos a la verdadera religión,* trans. Agustín Millares Carlo (Mexico City: Fondo de Cultura Económica, 1942), 7. This Spanish translation with facing Latin text is the first published editon of Las Casas's *De unico vocationis modo.* In the text I refer to Las Casas's work by its original Latin title, *De unico vocationis modo.* However, quotations are from Millares Carlo's Spanish translation and, therefore, the citations are to the published Spanish title, *Del único modo.*
14. Antonio de Remesal, O.P., *Historia general de las Indias Occidentales y particular de la Gobernación de Chiapa Guatemala,* ed. P. Carmelo Saenz de Santa Maria, S.J., in *Biblioteca de autores españoles* (Madrid: Atlas, 1964), 175:209.
15. Ibid.

16. Ibid.
17. *Del único modo*, 47.
18. II.xxvii.115.
19. I.ii.2–3.
20. *Del único modo*, 101.
21. The text of the bull appears in *De único modo*, 365–67. I have followed the translation of Martínez, "Las Casas on the Conquest of America," 316.
22. Ibid., 249.
23. Ibid.
24. Ibid., 255.
25. Ibid., 263.
26. Ibid., 459.
27. Remesal, *Historia general*, 211–12.
28. *Del único modo*, 503.
29. For a discussion of the the *Tercero catecismo*, see Juan Guillermo Duran, *El catecismo del III concilio provincial de Lima y sus complementos pastorales (1584– 1585)* (Buenos Aires: Editorial El Derecho, 1982), 239–55.
30. *Tercero catecismo*, in *Doctrina Christiana y catecismo para instruccion de indios, Corpus Hispanorum de Pace*, ed. Luciano Pereña (Madrid: Consejo Superior de Investigaciones Científicas, 1985), 26-2:353. This volume contains facsimile reproductions of several sixteenth-century missionary works. For the *Tercero catecismo*, see 333ff.
31. *De procuranda indorum salute, Corpus Hispanorum de Pace*, ed. Luciano Pereña et al. (Madrid: Consejo Superior de Investigaciones Científicas, 1984), 23:55.
32. *De procuranda*, 57, 59.
33. Ibid., 59.
34. Ibid., 63.
35. Ibid., 63–65.
36. Ibid., 67. Acosta does not cite Cicero at this point. Rather, he invokes the authority of Aristotle, *Politics*, 1254a.13–16.
37. Ibid., 67.
38. Ibid., 151
39. Ibid., 303–9.
40. Ibid., 321.
41. Ibid.
42. Ibid., 303. Acosta's opposition to a "just war" against barbarians is presented in bk. 2, chaps. 2–7.
43. Ibid.
44. *Tercero catecismo*, 354–55.
45. *De procuranda*, 141, 155.
46. *Tercero catecismo*, 355.
47. Ibid.

48. *Sacred Rhetoric*, 7.

49. *De procuranda*, 143, 139–41.

50. Ibid., 141.

51. *Symbolo Catholico Indiano, en el Qual se Declaran los Mysterios de la fe en tres Symbolos Catholicos, Apostolico, Niceno, y de S. Athanasio. Contiene assi mesmo una Descripción del nuevo orbe, y de los naturales del. Y un orden de enseñarles la doctrina Christiana en dos lenguas Generales Quichua Y Aymara, con un Confessionario breve y Catechismo de la Communion*, ff. 67–72. I have omitted the latter portion of the poem. The translation is that of Antonine Tibesar, *Franciscan Beginnings in Colonial Peru* (Washington, D.C.: Academy of American Franciscan History, 1953), 81.

52. *Tercero catecismo*, 355.

53. Ibid., 356.

54. Ibid.

55. Ibid.

56. *De procuranda*, 365. Acosta cites *De doctrina christiana*, 4.15.32.

57. *De procuranda*, 365–67.

58. Ibid., 365.

59. For Acosta's views on the *encomienda*, see esp. *De procuranda*, bk. 3, chap. 11. Virtually all of book 3 is devoted to a consideration of the civil administration of the Spanish colonies.

60. Ibid., 371.

61. *De procuranda*, 375.

62. Ibid.

63. Ibid., 377.

64. Ibid., 155, 157.

65. Ibid., 369.

Chapter 5

El Inca Garcilaso de la Vega
Renaissance Rhetoric and Native Narrative

Garcilaso de la Vega and Diego Valadés led what were in many respects parallel lives. Both were born in the New World to Spanish fathers and native mothers, both were exposed to European learning and to indigenous traditions, both wrote important literary works, and both lived their final years in the Old World. Despite these parallels, Garcilaso and Valadés differ in important regards. Valadés identified so thoroughly with the Europe of his father and of the Franciscans that there is virtually no acknowledgment in the *Rhetorica Christiana* of his dual heritage. His voice is always that of the missionary preaching to the Indians of New Spain. Garcilaso, on the other hand, was agonizingly aware that he was the issue of two cultures and that, as a mestizo, he was often estranged from both. Thus, he wrote not as a European apostle to the other but, instead, as a mestizo missionary to the land of his father.

Garcilaso and Valadés were both well versed in Renaissance rhetoric, but, because they conceived of the self and the other quite differently, they employed rhetoric in distinct ways. The *Rhetorica Christiana* is a preaching manual that, despite Valadés's Mexican birth and his narrative of indigenous customs, can be readily placed within the European rhetorical tradition. Although Garcilaso did not write a rhetoric manual, he was influenced by the rhetorical tradition, and his works are models of the rhetorician's art. His major works, *La Florida* and the *Comentarios reales* (including its second part, often called the *Historia general del Perú*), are not books about how to sermonize but are themselves sermonic. These works are also a part of Garcilaso's campaign to persuade the Spanish, and especially the Spanish monarchy, of the virtues of his Incan ancestors and the abilities of the new race of mestizos. His efforts to argue his case before a Spanish audience were largely shaped by his understanding of humanist literature in general and his mastery of Renaissance rhetoric in particular.

While Garcilaso tailored his style and arguments to the expectations of a European audience, he drew his material from his life as a Peruvian. Perhaps even more than Valadés, Garcilaso's writings always contain important biographical ingredients.[1] Garcilaso was born in Cuzco, the former Incan capital, in 1539. His father was Captain Sebastián Garcilaso de la Vega y Vargas, a Spaniard of noble lineage. His mother, Chimpu Ocllo, was the second cousin of Huáscar and Atahualpa, the last two claimants to the imperial title of Inca. Garcilaso was, therefore, the product of the nobility of Peru's old and new cultures; his awareness of his dual nobility figures prominently in his writings. He was baptized Gómez Suárez de Figueroa, a name also borne by his uncle and great grandfather. Only much later, while in Spain, would he assume the name Garcilaso de la Vega, in order to identify himself more closely with his father's family and his distant relative, the great Spanish poet Garcilaso de la Vega (1501?–1536). Later still he would add the royal appellation "the Inca" to indicate kinship with his Andean, as well as European, ancestors.

Relatively little is known about his education, but it is clear that early in his life Garcilaso was exposed to the traditions of both his father's and mother's people. He apparently grew up speaking first Quechua then Spanish and later learned some Latin in Cuzco. In 1560 he left Peru for Spain, probably with the intention to continue his education in Europe. His father had died the year before this departure, and thus Garcilaso may also have intended to claim compensation from the crown for his father's service in Peru. After arriving in Spain, Garcilaso spent some time in Seville, perfecting his Latin under the guidance of Pedro Sánchez de Herrera. In 1561 he went to the Andalusian town of Montilla, the home of his father's eldest brother. Garcilaso, supported by a modest income from family estates, would spend nearly thirty years of his life in Montilla. It was in this small town that Garcilaso began to develop a serious interest in literary matters. In 1590 he moved to Córdoba, where the literary efforts begun in Montilla were to be fully realized. The Inca spent the final years of his life in Córdoba. Garcilaso died in 1616 and was buried in the great cathedral of Córdoba.

During his years in Montilla and Córdoba, Garcilaso acquired a rather thorough command of Renaissance learning through his own efforts and through interaction with the intellectuals of those communities. The extent of Garcilaso's erudition may be surmised from the contents of the library he had accumulated at the time of his death. The inventory of this library reveals a respectable collection of classical and

Renaissance works of philosophy, religion, history, poetry, and rhetoric. Works in the later category include Aristotle's *Rhetoric,* a *De arte dicendi* identified as perhaps that of Juan Luis Vives and the *De arte rhetorica* of Francisco de Castro (1611).[2] Castro was a friend of Garcilaso, and his rhetoric is dedicated to the Inca.

The truest indicator, of course, of Garcilaso's mastery of Renaissance scholarship are the three books he wrote during his years in Montilla and Córdoba. The first of these, the *Diálogos de amor* (1590), is a translation from the Italian of León Hebreo's *Dialoghi d'amore.* Garcilaso's translation, widely regarded as a skillful rendering of the Italian text, served as an initiation into the difficult endeavors of Renaissance humanism. As Donald G. Castanien indicates, Garcilaso's translation proved an admirable beginning to a literary career: "The intellectual exercise for him consisted of the problem of converting as closely as possible all the thought of the original into another language, a task that demands constant interpretation of the first text. To accomplish it, the good translator must have excellent command of both languages involved, and equally important, he must have understanding of the material he is translating. The quality of the finished product as an example of the translator's art will depend upon the degree to which the translator has control of his materials."[3]

The translation of the *Diálogos de amor* proved to be a harbinger of the more original compositions that were to follow from the pen of the Inca. Garcilaso's reputation as one of the first Americans to produce literature recognized by Europeans derives not from his translation of the *Dialogues* but, rather, from his narratives of the New World: *The Florida of the Inca* and the *Royal Commentaries of the Incas and the General History of Peru.* Although it is in the *Royal Commentaries* that the influence of rhetoric is most clearly apparent, *The Florida* marks the true beginning of Garcilaso's career as a historian and rhetorician.

The Florida of the Inca

Garcilaso's first original work was published in 1605 under the title *The Florida of the Inca: A History of the Adelantado, Hernando de Soto, Governor and Captain General of the kingdom of Florida, and of other heroic Spanish and Indian cavaliers, written by The Inca, Garcilaso de la Vega, an officer of His Majesty, and a native of the great city of Cuzco, capital of the realms and provinces of Peru.*[4] As the title indicates, *The Florida* is a narrative of the explorations of de Soto through what was to become the southeastern United States. Garcilaso renders the six-year expedition of de Soto and his men into an extraordinary adventure in the tradition of the chivalry books and epics of medieval and Renaissance Europe.

Garcilaso began the project that ultimately became *The Florida* more than twenty years before its publication in 1605. *The Florida* was the result of a long collaboration between Garcilaso and "a great and noble friend," whom Garcilaso never identifies. This friend is now known to have been Gonzalo Silvestre, a hidalgo who had accompanied de Soto and with whom Garcilaso had become acquainted in Spain. Garcilaso says that *The Florida* was the result of urging his friend "to record the details of the expedition, using me as his amanuensis."[5] Thus, it might appear that Garcilaso's literary career progressed from translator to literary assistant. Garcilaso is being disingenuous, however, for *The Florida* is as much, if not more, his as that of his source. It is in *The Florida* that Garcilaso's literary talent is first fully displayed.

It is also in *The Florida* that Garcilaso first demonstrates his talents as a rhetorician, for his narrative of de Soto's expedition is unabashedly rhetorical in purpose and in execution. Garcilaso's explicitly stated purpose is to persuade the Spanish crown to undertake the colonization and Christianization of Florida. In his preface Garcilaso says that his and his collaborator's intent "in offering this description has been to encourage Spain to make an effort to acquire and populate this kingdom . . . even if, without the principal idea of augmenting the Holy Catholic Faith, she should carry forward the project for the sole purpose of establishing colonies to which she might send her sons to reside just as the ancient Romans did when there was no longer space in their native land."[6] For Garcilaso colonization, although always important, remains secondary to the diffusion of Christianity. Because he takes evangelization so seriously, Garcilaso insists he would never resort to fabrications in his account. Garcilaso fears he would "displease gravely the Eternal Majesty (who is the one we should fear most), if with the idea of inciting and persuading Spaniards by my history to acquire the land of Florida for the augmentation of Our Holy Catholic Faith, I should deceive with fictions and falsehoods those of them who might wish to employ their property and their life in such an undertaking. For indeed, to tell the whole truth, I have been moved to labor and to record this history solely by a desire to see Christianity extended to that land which is so broad and so long."[7]

Garcilaso's explicit purpose, persuading the crown to expand Spanish and Catholic domains by colonizing and evangelizing the lands explored by de Soto, is accompanied by another design, less explicit but
equally important to him. Garcilaso intends to create in the minds of his
Spanish audience an image of the Indians as civilized human beings.
He recalls that, upon hearing his "collaborator recount the very illustrious deeds that both Spaniards and Indians performed in the process of
the conquest, I became convinced that when such heroic actions as these
had been performed in this world, it was unworthy and regrettable that
they should remain in perpetual oblivion. Feeling myself under obligation to two races, since I am the son of a Spanish father and an Indian
mother, I many times urged this cavalier to record the details of the expedition."[8] Thus, Garcilaso, with a clear sense of duty, is determined to
demonstrate the error of those Spaniards who held the indigenes of the
New World inferior to Europeans or even altogether subhuman.

The very fact that Garcilaso, a Peruvian, could successfully execute
such a literary task is in itself eloquent evidence of the capacity of the
natives of the New World. Garcilaso pleads that

> this account be received in the same spirit as I present it, and that I be
> pardoned its errors because I am an Indian. For since we Indians are
> a people who are ignorant and uninstructed in the arts and sciences,
> it seems ungenerous to judge our deeds and utterances strictly in ac-
> cordance with the precepts of those subjects which we have not
> learned. We should be accepted as we are. And although I may not
> deserve such esteem, it would be a noble and magnanimous idea to
> carry this merciful consideration still further and to honor in me all
> of the mestizo Indians and the creoles of Peru, so that seeing a novice
> of their own race receive the favor and grace of the wise and learned,
> they would be encouraged to make advancements with similar ideas
> drawn from their own uncultivated mental resources.[9]

Thus, the principal deficiency of the New World's natives is their
lack of exposure to European learning and, most importantly, Christianity. Garcilaso attributes this ignorance of Christianity to the inad-
equacy of the Spanish mission rather than to the Amerindians' reluctance
to accept the true religion.

Garcilaso's Floridians are entirely the equal of the Spaniards in wisdom and heroism. These Indians are brave, proud, compassionate, and

remarkably eloquent. They frequently give stirring speeches, which Garcilaso is able to record exactly. The Inca recognizes that his readers may be skeptical of both the Indian's oratorical abilities and his own capacity to present their precise words. He therefore interrupts his narrative to rebut those who may harbor such doubts: "it will be well to answer an objection which could be raised to the effect that such deeds and speeches of the Indians as I relate here are not to be found in other histories of the West Indies. For in general these people are looked upon as a simple folk without reason or understanding who in both peace and war differ very little from beasts and accordingly could not do or say things so worthy of memory or praise as some of those things I have described up to this point. . . . Thus I may be accused of having written as I have either to fictionalize or to lavish praise upon my own people."[10]

Garcilaso argues that his account may seem outlandish to some only because most information about the Indians is entirely unreliable. He refers his readers to Acosta's *Historia natural y moral del Nuevo Orbe* for an accurate assessment of the peoples of the New World. As for himself, Garcilaso says he "contributed no more than the pen, and can truthfully declare that this account is not a fabric of my imagination." His own account, he says, is derived from a very reliable eyewitness, who related the events to Garcilaso and then carefully edited the manuscript. Garcilaso insists that "in fact all my life I have been an enemy of such fiction as one finds in books of Knighthood and the like, good poetry excepted."[11] He is especially indignant that he should be suspected of exaggerating the accomplishments of the natives because of the circumstances of his birth. Garcilaso says he lacks the ability to exaggerate even if he were so inclined: "I confess with shame on my part that instead of finding myself with an excess of words to overstate what did not occur, I lack sufficient words to present in their proper light the actual truths that are offered me in this history. Such a deficiency is a result of the unfortunate circumstances of my childhood, for at that time there were no schools of letters and there was an excess of schools of arms for training both infantry and cavalry."[12] Garcilaso concludes that he and his informant had simply written the truth "not with an excess of hyperbole but rather with a lack of the eloquence and rhetoric necessary to give the deeds their proper place of honor."[13] His disclaimer, conventionally disingenuous, is intended to assure readers that the eloquence attributed to the Indians is indeed their own and not of Garcilaso's invention.

The Florida is a plea for the dignity and the humanity of the natives of the New World. The considerable virtues of the Floridians are exhibited in their actions and in their frequent orations. Despite Garcilaso's sympathetic portrayal of the indigenous peoples, *The Florida* is a story of European exploration. Garcilaso is an Indian, but these are not his people, nor was he an eyewitness to the events he describes. In *The Florida* Garcilaso writes at a distance from his subject; although more than the amanuensis he claims to be, he is far from a participant in the narrative. Thus, in *The Florida* Garcilaso does not have the authority, the ethos, and therefore the rhetorical efficacy, which he will achieve in his final and greatest work.

Royal Commentaries of the Incas

In the *Royal Commentaries of the Incas* Garcilaso is no longer translating another's treatise or telling someone else's story. The *Royal Commentaries* is his story, the narrative of his two peoples, the Incas and the Spaniards, and it is his masterpiece. The *Royal Commentaries,* truly grand in scope, is presented in two long volumes. The first volume is entitled *Part One of the Royal Commentaries which treat[s] of the origins of the Incas, the former kings of Peru, their idolatry, laws, and government in peace and war, and of their lives and conquests, and everything relating to that empire and its society before the arrival of the Spaniards. Written by the Inca Garcilaso de la Vega, a native of Cuzco, and a captain in His Majesty's service.* This work was followed in 1617 by part 2, which bears the title *General History of Peru which treats of its discovery and of how the Spaniards conquered it; the civil wars between the Pizarros and the Almagros about the partition of the land; the rising of various rebels and their punishment; and other particular events that are comprised in the history.*[14] As the two titles make clear, the *Royal Commentaries* first traces the development of the Incas from their mythic beginnings to their subjugation by the Spanish and then chronicles the disastrous consequences of the Spanish domination of Peru.

The representation of the wisdom and eloquence of the indigenous peoples which Garcilaso first presented in the *The Florida* is continued and amplified in the *Royal Commentaries.* Because he is writing about his ancestors, and his family, he naturally identifies more closely with his subjects than he did in the earlier work; no longer the amanuensis, Garcilaso is now the participant. That he is the "Inca," of course, furnishes him with an ethos he could not claim in *The Florida*. This familiarity with the oral narratives of the Incas gives the *Royal Commentaries* an intimacy and a legitimacy that few other chronicles of colonial Peru possess. Garcilaso claims that he will "simply tell the tales he imbibed with my mother's milk," along with those accounts furnished at his request by his former schoolmates in Peru.[15] He supplements these oral traditions and letters from native informants with the work of earlier Spanish chroniclers.[16] His most important written source is a history of Peru written by the Jesuit Blas Valera, which is now known only through the pages of the *Royal Commentaries*.

As he was in *The Florida*, Garcilaso is again concerned that his account should be accepted by his readers as credible. Although much of what he reports is derived from his relatives, he promises that "my affection for them shall not cause me to stray from the true facts either by underestimating the ill or exaggerating the good they did." He promises, "I shall not write new and unheard of things, but will recount the same things the Spanish historians have written of those parts and their kings, bringing forward where necessary their very words, so as to prove that I have not invented fictitious circumstances to the credit of my relatives, but say no more than what Spaniards have said."[17] Garcilaso modestly maintains that he will be no more than a commentator on the chronicles of Peru already written by Spanish historians.

Immediately after claiming to be merely a commentator, however, he begins to reveal a rather different purpose. He says that "much will be added that is missing in their histories but really happened."[18] The omissions from and distortions in the Spanish histories resulted from the Spaniard's inability to engage in meaningful communication with the Incas. Indeed, a central theme of the *Royal Commentaries* is the tragic consequences of failed communication. Garcilaso, of course, has the advantage over other chroniclers because he knows Quechua, the "general language of Peru." His account of the rise of the Incas is translated "faithfully from my mother tongue, that of the Inca, into a foreign speech, Castilian."[19] The bilingual and bicultural Garcilaso is dismissive of those Europeans who claim to know the native tongue: "the Spaniard who thinks he knows the language best is ignorant of nine-tenths of it."[20] Thus, far from providing a mere commentary on Spanish histories, Garcilaso intends the *Royal Commentaries* as a corrective to the distortions and omissions of the available chronicles. Garcilaso the historian is intent on rehabilitating the history of the Incas, and he is in a singular position to do so.

Garcilaso the rhetorician, however, is concerned with much more than historical accuracy. Rather, he seeks to persuade his Spanish audience, and especially the Spanish crown, to radically alter colonial policy in Peru. Garcilaso's efforts in the *Royal Commentaries* are not unlike his earlier attempt in *The Florida* to convince the Spanish to undertake the colonization and Christianization of a neglected corner of the empire. His effort in the *Royal Commentaries* is far more delicate and difficult than that of *The Florida*. Garcilaso must convince his readers that the administration of Spain's richest colony is nothing less than a disaster for Peruvians and Spaniards alike. Moreover, the cause of this disaster is the Spaniard's inability to communicate with, and hence understand, the civilization of the Incas. Spanish ignorance permitted the destruction of the Incan state, which in turn precipitated the decline of the entire colony of Peru.

The implication of this thesis, of course, is that the political organization and the cultural accomplishments of the Incas are actually superior to Spanish institutions and traditions. Not surprisingly, Garcilaso is reluctant to advocate such a position explicitly. Rather, he proceeds by carefully contrived insinuation: "in all that I shall have to say about a state that was destroyed before it had been known, I shall plainly tell everything concerning its idolatry, rites, sacrifices, and ceremonies in ancient times, and its government, laws, and customs in peace and war, and make no comparison with other histories divine or human, nor with the government of our times, for all comparisons are odious."[21] Although Garcilaso eschews comparisons, he invites the reader to "make his own comparisons, for he will find many points of similarity in ancient history, both in Holy Writ and in the profane histories and fables of ancient antiquity. He will observe many laws and customs that compare with those of our own age and hear many others quite contrary to them."[22] With Garcilaso's assistance the reader cannot avoid comparing the two Perus of the Incas and the Spaniards, and the comparisons are odious indeed. In virtually all regards the Incas are not merely the equal of the Spanish; they are superior. The only exception is religion; Garcilaso has no doubts that Christianity is the only acceptable religion. It is, for him, the justification for Spanish domination, and he is especially distressed that the foolishness of imperial policy has retarded the legitimate mission of evangelization.

Garcilaso builds his case on behalf of the Incas and against the Spanish through a neatly fashioned parallel structure. Part 1 of the *Royal Commentaries* chronicles the Incan empire of Tahuantinsuyu; part 2 recounts the Spanish viceroyalty of Peru. Under the tutelage of the Incas, Peru ascends from barbarity to civilization. Under the bondage of the Spanish the process reverses: Peru descends from civilization back into barbarity. Garcilaso seems to recognize that the Incan state cannot be restored to its preconquest conditions. His alternative to the colonial arrangement appears to be a Peru both Incan and Christian under the distant and benevolent suzerainty of the Spanish crown. Thus, the *Royal Commentaries* are at once both historical and rhetorical; by preserving the past and correcting the record, Garcilaso seeks to influence the future.[23]

In constructing the Incas' past, Garcilaso is guided by one of the most persistent images of Renaissance rhetoric: the Ciceronian vision of the civilizing power of discourse. Garcilaso, like Valadés, appropriates Cicero's account in *De inventione* of the beginning of civilization, when humans were lifted from brutishness to civilization by a man "great and eloquent." Unlike Valadés, however, Garcilaso does not invoke this image to demonstrate the possibility of civilizing the New World's natives by discursive means. Garcilaso's purpose is fundamentally different. He appropriates the Ciceronian motif to demonstrate that the Incas are civilized and that their cultural development parallels the course of classical European civilization.

Garcilaso begins his account of the Incas at the very same place at which Cicero commences his explanation of the accomplishments of the Romans. From the beginning of part 1 of the *Royal Commentaries* Garcilaso invites his readers to compare the Incan empire with the Roman. So, Garcilaso begins his narrative at a time when, as Cicero says, "men wandered at large in the fields like animals."[24] Garcilaso's narrative, however, immediately surpasses the Roman account, which is brief and perfunctory. Cicero is anxious to get on with explaining the intricacies of rhetorical invention, whereas Garcilaso's task of defending the humanity of a subjugated people to an imperialist audience requires a more complete narrative. The suggestive paragraph in *De inventione* is insufficient for Garcilaso's purposes. Cicero could assume that readers would acquiesce to what had by his time already become something of a cultural myth. Garcilaso, in contrast, devotes several chapters of the *Royal Commentaries* to this theme because he must achieve a verisimilitude in order to be persuasive.

Garcilaso divides his account of the native peoples of Peru into two parts: before the coming of the Incas and after. The period before the Incas corresponds to the primeval time described by Cicero in *De inventione.* Garcilaso says that it must be realized that in "the first age of primitive heathendom," that is, before the arrival of the Incas, "there were Indians who were little better than tame beasts and others much worse than wild beasts." The gods of these Indians "were of a piece with the simplicity and the stupidity of the times, as regards the multiplicity of gods and the vileness and crudity of the things the people worshipped."[25] Garcilaso tells his readers that these Indians "worshipped grasses, plants, flowers, trees of all kinds, high hills, great rocks and nooks in them, deep caves, pebbles, and little pieces of stone of various colors found in rivers and streams."[26] The variety of gods was exceeded by the cruelty of sacrificial practices of these people. Garcilaso claims that, in addition to the sacrifice of such ordinary things as animals and the fruits of the earth, "they sacrificed men and women of all ages taken captive in the wars they waged on one another. . . . Not satisfied with sacrificing their captive foes, in case of need they offered up their own children."[27]

These barbarians "lived in huts scattered over the fields, valleys and river bottoms," and, like the primitive Europeans described by Cicero, "the ruler was whoever was boldest and had the will to govern the rest. As soon as he became master, he treated his vassals tyrannically and cruelly, using them as slaves, taking their wives and daughters, and making war on his rivals."[28] These barbarous conditions were compounded by the great variety of languages spoken: "each district, each tribe, and, in many places, each village had its own language, differing from that of its neighbors. Those who could understand one another in one language regarded themselves as relatives and thus were friends and allies. Those who did not understand one another because of the variety of languages, held one another as enemies and opposites, and waged cruel war and even ate one another as if they were beasts of different kinds."[29] Finally, then, and most despicably, Garcilaso maintains that many of the Indians practiced all manner of cannibalism, which he describes in gruesome detail. One tribe, he claims, was "so strongly addicted to devouring human flesh" that, "as soon as the deceased had breathed his last, his relatives gathered round and ate him roasted or boiled."[30]

Garcilaso's description of the Peruvian tribes before the arrival of the Incas confirms the popular European images of the Amerindians as creatures who lived like animals, worshiped inanimate objects indiscriminately, were ruled by force rather than law, and ate parents and children without remorse. Moreover, he does so in vivid detail. Margarita Zamora observes that the early chapters of the *Royal Commentaries* are replete with the device of amplification: "The multiplication of subordinate clauses which serve to amplify the semantic kernel of each sentence also contributes to overwhelming the reader with a baroque proliferation of variants on a constant theme which rises in a crescendo of iniquities and peaks in a lusty feast of cannibalism, whose horrific effect is intensified by the occasional infanticide."[31] In these early chapters Garcilaso illustrates the conviction of Renaissance rhetoricians that amplification is powerful. It is almost as if he is confirming Luis de Granada's contention in the *Ecclesiasticae rhetoricae* that it is amplification that creates belief. In particular, what Garcilaso establishes in these chapters is a vivid contrast between the barbarism of the pre-Incan tribes and the sophisticated civilization of the Incas themselves.

As a boy in Cuzco, Garcilaso had been told of the rise of the Incas by his mother's relatives. Although he had heard these stories many times in his childhood, it was not until he was sixteen or seventeen that he began to appreciate the significance of these traditions to the Incan way of life. In his adolescence Garcilaso asked his uncle, whom he identifies only as "the Inca," to tell the tale of their common ancestors. His uncle was only too happy to oblige. The Inca begins his narrative by telling Garcilaso, "you should know that in olden times the whole of this region before you was covered with brush and heath, and people lived in those times like wild beasts, with no religion or government and no towns or houses, and without tilling or sowing the soil, or clothing or covering their flesh."[32] The Inca's initial response serves as a brief summary of the preceding chapters and yet another indication, should any reader have failed to notice, of the parallel origins of the Incan and Roman empires.

The beastly existence of the inhabitants of the Peruvian highlands begins to change with the arrival of the first Inca, Manco Cápac. Manco Cápac had been sent by the god of the Sun to create an orderly society. Here Garcilaso's narrative diverges from the Ciceronian by introducing a divine direction in the process of civilizing in contrast to the rational and entirely human process imagined by Cicero. The divine origin of the Incas is important to Garcilaso's argument that the Inca's monotheistic sun worship prepared the natives of Peru ultimately to accept Christianity. Thus, Manco Cápac set out to civilize the barbarians around him, and he did so in a manner much like the Cicero's great and wise man, by persuasion rather than by force. The Inca instructed the Indians "in the urbane, social, and brotherly conduct they were to use toward one another according to the dictates of reason and natural law, effectively persuading them to do unto one another as they themselves would be done by, so that there should be perpetual peace and concord among them."[33]

Garcilaso maintains that the Inca created a civilization and an empire primarily by the force of persuasion and only secondarily by the force of arms. Garcilaso notes that, "among other things devised by the Inca kings for the good government of their empire, they bade all their vassals learn the language of their capital, which is what is now called the general language."[34] As a result of this policy, the various tribes subjugated by the Incas put aside their religious and cultural differences and came "to love one another as if they were of the same family and kinship by talking and revealing their inmost hearts to one another, thus losing the fear that arises from not understanding each other."[35] Not only does knowledge of the Quechua enhance intertribal communication, but, says Garcilaso, the Indians who learn it "seem themselves nobler, more cultured, and of better understanding."[36] Ultimately, mastery of the general language makes those who know it "keener in understanding and more tractable and ingenious in what they learn, turning them from savages into civilized and conversible men."[37] He cannot resist a comparison: Quechua "has the same value to the Peruvian Indians as Latin to us."[38] Although Garcilaso does not say so explicitly, the Incan experience confirms Nebrija's dictum that language is the perfect instrument of empire.

Indeed, it is remarkable how often in Garcilaso's account the Incas recognized and practiced the ideals of Renaissance humanism. In particular, they understood the inextricable link between language and civilization as well as the practical advantages of a common language that transcended the babel of innumerable vernaculars. In this respect, as in many others, the Incas are depicted by Garcilaso as the Romans of the New World. Ironically, the Spanish, themselves heirs to the Roman world, did not appreciate the link between language and empire nearly so well as the Incas. Garcilaso laments that after the Spanish conquest the knowledge of the general language declined and the linguistic confusion of pre-Incan times returned, to the detriment of both civil authority and the evangelical mission.[39] Garcilaso quotes Father Blas Valera: "it is a pity that the work done by these barbarian pagans to dispel the confusion of tongues, in which they succeeded so well with their industry and skill, should have been so neglected by us, despite its value for teaching the Indians the doctrine of Our Lord Jesus Christ."[40]

Garcilaso rejects the imposition of Spanish as an alternative to Quechua, a proposal that "arises more from the weakness of spirit than from dullness of understanding."[41] Garcilaso believes that Quechua, still widely if imperfectly known under Spanish domination, and close to other indigenous tongues, is uniquely suited to the task of evangelization. The Indians who speak the general language, Garcilaso maintains, "grow better adapted to receive the doctrine of the Catholic Faith, and of course preachers who know this tongue well take pleasure in standing up to discuss higher things, feeling that they can explain them to their hearers without the slightest trepidation, for just as the Indians who speak this tongue are of keener and more capacious intelligence, so also the language itself has greater scope and a wider variety of elegant ornaments." In this first part of the *Royal Commentaries* the Spanish unwillingness to employ the general language of Cuzco signals a broader lack of appreciation for the importance of language in affairs human and divine. The Incas, in contrast, understood this very well, and, as a result, Garcilaso's readers are left with the impression that it is the Incas, not the Spanish, who truly conformed to the Renaissance appreciation of eloquence.

In the second part of the *Royal Commentaries* the inability of the Spanish to communicate with the Incas, and thus the impossibility of their engaging in persuasion, has predictable and tragic results. The Spanish contempt for communication is most vividly presented by Garcilaso in an episode early in part 2, and indeed a crucial moment in the conquest of Peru: the meeting between the Spanish captain Francisco Pizarro and the Incan emperor Atahuallpa at Cajamarca. Pizarro was accompanied by about 160 men, Atahuallpa by a entourage of several thousand lords, dignitaries, and soldiers. Fray Vicente Valverde, a Dominican friar accompanying Pizarro's expedition, was selected to address Atahuallpa. Valverde's speech was brief and divided into two parts. In the first part Valverde explains, in three paragraphs, the basic tenets of Christian doctrine. In the next section he describes the duty of the pope and the emperor Charles V to bring the benefits of Christianity to all the world. Valverde then concludes by indicating that Charles' lieutenant, Pizarro, is present in Peru to bestow these same benefits upon Atahuallpa. Specifically, Valverde proclaims that Pizarro will "establish a league and alliance of perpetual friendship between His Majesty and Your Highness and all your realms will become tributaries; that is to say, you will pay tribute to the emperor, and will become his vassal and deliver your kingdom wholly into his hands, renouncing the administration and government of it, as other kings and lords have done."[42] Valverde concludes by advising Atahuallpa to accept this attractive proposal willingly, for, "if you refuse, know that you will be constrained with war, fire, and the sword, and all your idols shall be overthrown and we shall oblige you by the sword to abandon your false religion and to receive willy-nilly our catholic faith and pay tribute to our emperor and deliver him your kingdom."[43]

Garcilaso rightly observes that Valverde's speech "was short and harsh, with no touch of softness."[44] Unfortunately, says Garcilaso, "the interpretation was much worse" because Valverde's interpreter, an "Indian dragoman" called Felipe, was accomplished in neither Quechua nor Castilian.[45] Felipe was "a man of very plebeian origins" who had learned the general language not in Cuzco but in the coastal town of Túmbez, "from Indians who speak barbarously and corruptly."[46] His knowledge of Spanish was even worse, because, having learned it by listening to the conversations of common soldiers, his vocabulary consisted almost entirely of expletives.

Garcilaso records that Atahuallpa, naturally dismayed at the severity of Valverde's speech, nevertheless responded in a dignified manner. His first concern was not with the threats of the Spaniards but, rather, with their inability to communicate with him in an intelligible and elegant manner. Atahuallpa begins his reply to Valverde:

> It would have caused me great satisfaction, since you deny everything else that I requested of your messengers, that you should at least have granted me one request, that of addressing me through a more skilled and faithful translator. For the urbanity and social life of men is more readily understood through speech than by customs, since even though you may be endowed with great virtues, if you do not manifest them by words, I shall not easily be able to perceive them by observation and experience. And if this is needful among all peoples and nations, it is much more so between those who come from such widely different regions as we; if we seek to deal and talk through interpreters and messengers who are ignorant of both languages it will be as though we were conversing through the mouths of beasts of burden.[47]

In contrast to the harshness of Valverde, Atahuallpa is conciliatory, and, in the interests of effective expression, the Inca presents his speech slowly, in sections, using a dialect with which Felipe was more likely to be familiar. While the Inca was making every effort at clear expression, the Spanish were growing impatient with Atahuallpa's oratory. Finally, says Garcilaso, the Spaniards, "who were unable to brook the length of the discourse, had left their places and fallen on the Indians."[48]

The scene suddenly shifts from civil discourse to bloody warfare. In the ensuing battle Atahuallpa was captured by Pizarro, and the Spanish killed, by Garcilaso's estimate, some five thousand of Atahuallpa's followers. Not long after this episode Pizarro ordered Atahuallpa executed. The events at Cajamarca mark the beginning of the end of the Incan empire. The remaining eight hundred or so pages of the *Royal Commentaries* are devoted to the Spanish conquerors: the consolidation of their rule, their civil wars, their exploitation of the Indians and the resultant revolts, as well as the exploits of the honorable Spaniards, including, most noticeably, Garcilaso's father.

The speeches of Valverde and Atahuallpa again invite readers to engage in the comparisons that Garcilaso says he will not make. Valverde's speech is stern and insensitive to the audience and, to make matters worse, translated by a barely literate peasant. In contrast, Atahuallpa's speech, cautious and conciliatory, reveals a respect for discourse completely absent from the Spanish camp. A heathen and a barbarian, Atahuallpa acts in concert with the beliefs of Renaissance humanism, while Christians, driven by greed, disregard civilized dialogue and act with utter barbarity.

By the end of the *Royal Commentaries* Garcilaso has achieved a complete reversal of what, to most sixteenth-century Spaniards, would appear to be the natural order of things. The presumed attributes of Spaniard and Inca, Christian and heathen, have been completely reversed. In affecting this role reversal, Garcilaso renders it difficult for even a Spanish reader not to suspect that Peru would be in better hands under Incan rule. He accomplishes this transference by employing the resources of rhetoric, both thematically and technically. The book begins with Garcilaso invoking the Ciceronian image of the orator as agent of civilization—an image that would have been familiar to most literate Europeans. The Incas create and disseminate their civilization by rhetorical means: they engage in civil discourse; they foster universal communication by spreading the "general language"; and they persuade the peoples around them to voluntarily join the Inca community.

Garcilaso not only employs the commonplaces of Renaissance rhetoric but the techniques as well. Perhaps no element of rhetoric is more thoroughly endorsed in Renaissance textbooks than the use of amplification as a means of creating belief. Garcilaso proves himself a master of *amplificatio* as he displays some fifteen hundred pages of details. Through his mastery of amplification Garcilaso creates a vivid world of Peru before and after the arrival of the Spanish. This marshaling of details enables Garcilaso to recreate for European readers a portrait of Peru of dramatic verisimilitude. It is difficult to imagine that Garcilaso could have achieved so compelling a picture of the New World without employing the rhetorical resources of the Old World.

Guaman Poma de Ayala

Garcilaso was not the only Peruvian to employ the resources of rhetoric in an effort to sway the Spanish crown on behalf of the colony. Such rhetorical strategies are especially evident in the work of Garcilaso's contemporary, the Andean native Felipe Guaman Poma de Ayala (ca.1535–ca.1615). Guaman Poma's *El primer nueva corónica y buen gobierno*,[49] completed about 1613, parallels in many ways Garcilaso's *Commentarios reales*. This *First New Chronicle and Good Government*, written as a letter to Philip III of Spain,[50] is "from cover to cover a rhetorical enterprise devoted to persuading the Spanish king to institute radical colonial reforms."[51]

Thus, Garcilaso and Guaman Poma are bound together in their rhetorical enterprise by a common, and very specific, conception of audience and a mutual conviction that Spain's failed Peruvian policy demands rehabilitation. As Andeans addressing a European monarch, they also share a vital need to establish their ethos if they are to have any hope of influencing their distant readers. Both, therefore, emphasize their noble ancestry and their intimate knowledge of native traditions and customs, which, taken together, endow their narratives with greater authenticity than a European could achieve. Despite, or perhaps because of, their New World births, both portray themselves as loyal to the crown and faithful to the church. Each wants a Christian Peru, and each, in different ways, argues that a Christian consciousness was present in Peru well before the arrival of Pizarro.

Despite the parallels between Garcilaso and Guaman Poma, the *Nueva corónica* and the *Commentarios reales* are very different endeavors.

Though both are Peruvians, Garcilaso is a mestizo and Guaman Poma an Indian. Garcilaso identified with his European ancestors and lived out his life in Spain; Guaman Poma lived and died in Peru. Garcilaso is the son of an Incan princess and credits his mother's people with bringing civilization to the Peruvian highlands; Guaman Poma claims descent from the Yarovilcas and dismisses the Incas as usurpers. Both argue for reforms, but each envisions a different Peru. The mestizo Garcilaso desires a hybrid society, whereas the Indian Guaman Poma regards the complete segregation of Spaniard and Andean as the only acceptable royal policy. Garcilaso mastered both classical and vernacular European languages and wrote complex narratives in them. Guaman Poma never became proficient in Spanish, though compelled by necessity to compose in it. His writing is interspersed throughout with words, phrases, and long interjections in Quechua. As a result, Guaman Poma's prose is as opaque and awkward as Garcilaso's is translucent and graceful.

Thus, it is not surprising that, while both Garcilaso and Guaman Poma are engaged in rhetorical enterprises, they differ in their understanding and application of rhetoric itself. Garcilaso was well acquainted with the rhetorical traditions and preceptive literature of the Renaissance. Guaman Poma probably did not study rhetoric, as did Garcilaso, but he certainly was exposed to it through the rhetorical practice of the missionaries in Peru. His rhetoric, therefore, was religious and propagandistic and is reflected in the sermonic character of the *Nueva corónica*.

Guaman Poma was not only familiar with Spanish sermonizing; he was also familiar with the missionary literature produced by the likes of Las Casas, Acosta, Oré, and especially Granada.[52] Adorno has demonstrated that the collections of *sermonarios* and *catecismos,* such as the *Tercero catecismo,* circulating in colonial Peru were very influential in shaping Guaman Poma's strategy as a writer.[53] The *Nueva corónica* is composed of a long series of short, thematic chapters, each of which is by followed by a "prologue" similar to a Spanish sermon. [54]

A significant portion of the *Nueva corónica* is devoted to Guaman Poma's description of the attitudes and behavior of Spanish colonialists, including priestly deportment. Included in this section is a discussion of sermons. Guaman Poma also employs sermons, or rather parodies of sermons, in the *Nueva corónica*. While parodies, they are skillful ones, and Guaman Poma captures the sentiments of the missionaries.[55] These show that Guaman Poma understood well the genre of the sermon.

The *Nueva corónica* is an important instance of the transition from the oral discourse of the Andeans to a written narrative in the European

manner.[56] Guaman Poma was conscious of the difficulty of this undertaking and attempted to compensate for his unfamiliarity with the written word by augmenting his text with some 456 of his own drawings.[57]
As Guaman Poma explains to his intended audience, the king: "I have
given greater clarity to the text by means of pictures and drawings, know-
ing your Majesty to be greatly addicted to these. I have also wished to
alleviate the dullness and annoyance likely to be caused by reading a
work so lacking in ornament and polished style, such as more distinguished writers devote to the preservation of the Catholic faith, the correction of errors and the salvation of souls."[58]

These illustrations provide much of the coherence of this long and
cumbersome work. The drawings do not simply give "greater clarity"
to his prose; they also direct the narrative itself. The prose follows the
pictures; the chapters serve as a commentary on Guaman Poma's drawings. The centrality of visual imagery in the *Nueva corónica* is a reflection
of the oral traditions of the Andeans. But the use of pictures also corresponds with Renaissance preaching practices in both Europe and the
New World. The *Nueva corónica* is an illustration of the process explained
by Valadés in the *Rhetorica Christiana* in which the preacher explicates
for his audience a series of linen screens. In the *Nueva corónica* Guaman
Poma assumes the role of the preacher, pointing in prose to his drawings and explaining their meanings to his readers.

It is understandable that Guaman Poma, exposed to the Spaniard's
sermons and catechisms, should choose to write in Spanish from the
perspective of a preacher. Preaching, the characteristic oral mode of the
new dominant culture, offered him a means to communicate with that
culture. In the *Nueva corónica* Guaman Poma demonstrates, perhaps even
more than does Garcilaso in the *Royal Commentaries*, the degree to which
rhetoric had become an essential implement of intercultural communication in the New World.

While both Guaman Poma and Garcilaso were intent on writing the
truth, the historical accuracy of the *Nueva corónica* and the *Royal Commentaries* have often been questioned. Certainly, in the *Nueva corónica*
history and myth are combined in a complex and confusing universe.[59]
But Guaman Poma, like Garcilaso, has little interest in, or appreciation
of, chronological accuracy.[60] Both, however, are vitally interested in truth.
For both, as rhetors, the past serves the needs of the present and the
future. They portray truth as they know it—the truth of failed Spanish
colonial policy and the truth of better options. In Garcilaso's case it is
unlikely that all Incan successes were the result of persuasion or that all

Spanish failures were the consequence of contempt for communication. But Garcilaso does provide a wealth of material about the lives of the Incas and the Spanish which has proven invaluable to historians who have followed the Inca. The *Royal Commentaries* shows the Incas at their best and the Spanish at their worst. Ultimately, Garcilaso's version of civilization and barbarity in Peru is perhaps not greatly distorted. He, like Guaman Poma, strives for a verisimilitude that will lead readers to a higher truth. But Garcilaso, far more than Guaman Poma, believes in the civilizing power of language. Although the Inca's *Royal Commentaries* is a confirmation of the consequences of failed communication, it is also a testament to the potential of discourse. Garcilaso offers a glimpse of how Peruvians and Spaniards, Americans and Europeans, are most civilized when they resort to rhetoric rather than force.

Notes

1. The most complete biography of Garcilaso is John Varner, *El Inca: The Life and Times of Garcilaso de la Vega* (Austin: University of Texas Press, 1968).

2. *De arte rhetorica dialogi quatuor.* Castro's dedication to his friend fills three pages of florid Latin. A Spanish translation of this dedication is included in Raúl Porras Barrenechea, *El Inca Garcilaso en Montilla* (Lima: Editorial San Marcos, 1955), 260–63.

3. *El Inca Garcilaso de la Vega* (New York: Twayne, 1969), 55.

4. All references are to the English translation of this work: *The Florida of the Inca,* ed. and trans. John Grier Varner and Jeanette Johnson Varner (Austin: University of Texas Press, 1951).

5. Ibid., xxxvii.

6. Ibid., xxxviii.

7. Ibid., xliii.

8. Ibid., xxxvii.

9. Ibid., xlv.

10. Ibid., 158.

11. Ibid.

12. Ibid., 159.

13. Ibid., 161.

14. This title was apparently imposed by censors in Madrid to avoid any suggestion that the Incas had any legitimate claim to a Peruvian throne. See Harold V. Livermore, "Introduction," *Royal Commentaries of the Incas and General History of Peru,* by El Inca Garcilaso de la Vega (Austin: University of Texas Press, 1966), pt. 2, xxvi.

15. *Royal Commentaries*, 51.

16. Garcilaso cites with particular frequencies the following: José de Acosta, *Historia natural y moral del Nuevo Mundo;* Pedro Cieza de León, *Crónica del Perú;* Francisco López de Gómara, *Historia general de las Indias;* and Agustín de Zárate, *Historia del descubrimiento y conquista del la provincia del Perú.*

17. *Royal Commentaries*, 51.

18. Ibid.

19. Ibid., 46.

20. Ibid., 51.

21. Ibid.

22. Ibid.

23. For a discussion of Garcilaso and Renaissance historiography, see Margarita Zamora, *Language, Authority, and Indigenous History in the* Commentarios reales de los incas (Cambridge: Cambridge University Press, 1988), esp. 12–61. A standard study of the relationship between rhetoric and history is Nancy Struever, *The Language of History in the Renaissance: Rhetoric and Historical Consciousness in Florentine Humanism* (Princeton: Princeton University Press, 1970).

24. *De inventione,* I.ii.2. Margarita Zamora argues, following the interpretation of Marcelino Menéndez y Pelayo, that Garcilaso's representation of the civilizing role of the Incas is strongly influenced by Thomas More's *Utopia.* It seems likely that Garcilaso was inspired by both More and Cicero. The affinity with Cicero would, of course, help establish the association between the Incas and the Romans. It is also likely that More was influenced by Cicero's widely known account of civilization's origins. See Zamora, *Language, Authority, and Indigenous History,* 129–65.

25. *Royal Commentaries*, 30.

26. Ibid., 31.

27. Ibid., 33.

28. Ibid., 35.

29. Ibid., 39.

30. Ibid., 37.

31. *Language, Authority, and Indigenous History,* 112.

32. *Royal Commentaries*, 43.

33. Ibid., 53.

34. Ibid., 403.

35. Ibid.

36. Ibid., 410.

37. Ibid.

38. Ibid.

39. Shirley Bryce Heath notes a similar situation in New Spain, where the Mexica had established Nahuatl as a common language among linguistically

diverse groups. The Spanish, however, failed to take advantage of this already funtioning "international" language. As Heath puts it: "The Conquistadors walked into a solution and made it a problem" (*Telling Tongues: Language Policy in Mexico—Colony to Nation* [New York: Columbia University; Teacher's College Press, 1972], 1). See Heath's first two chapters for a review of royal and ecclesiastical policies on language in colonial Mexico.

40. Ibid., 410.

41. Ibid., 407. Garcilaso is again quoting Blas Valera.

42. Ibid., 680.

43. Ibid., 680–81.

44. Ibid., 681.

45. Ibid.

46. Ibid., 681–82.

47. Ibid., 685.

48. Ibid., 687.

49. Ed. John V. Murra and Rolena Adorno, 3 vols. (Mexico City: Siglo XXI, 1980).

50. Juan Ossio argues that "Letter to the King" is a more accurate title than *The First New Chronicle and Good Government* ("Myth and History: The Seventeenth-Century Chronicle of Guaman Poma de Ayala," in *Text in Context: The Social Anthropology of Tradition,* ed. Ravinda K. Jain [Philadelphia: Institute for the Study of Human Issues, 1977], 51). Christopher Dilke rendered an abridged translation of the the *Nueva cronónica* as *Letter to a King* (New York: Dutton, 1987).

51. *Guaman Poma: Writing and Resistance in Colonial Peru* (Austin: University of Texas Press, 1986), 78. My analysis of the *Nueva Corónica* is indebted to Adorno's careful investigation into the rhetorical aspects of Guaman Poma's work. *Writing and Resistance in Colonial Peru* is one of the few studies to demonstrate the degree to which rhetoric had established itself in Spain's American colonies. See also her book *Cronista y príncipe: La obra de don Felipe Guaman Poma de Ayala* (Lima: Pontifical Catholic University of Peru, 1989).

52. Adorno has identified Granada as one of Guaman Poma's most important sources and the only one he specifically acknowledges (*Writing and Resistance,* 58). Irving Leonard's pioneering studies of the book trade in colonial Spanish America demonstrate that by the standards of the times Granada was a best-selling author in Peru. See "Don Quijote and the Book Trade in Lima, 1616," *Hispanic Review* 8 (1940): 285–304; "On the Cuzco Book Trade, 1606," *Hispanic Review* 9 (1941): 359–75; and "Best Sellers of the Lima Book Trade," *Hispanic American Historical Review* 22 (1942): 5–33.

53. *Writing and Resistance,* 57.

54. Ibid., 70–71.

55. *Nueva corónica,* 2:576–82.

56. *From Oral to Written Expression: Native Andean Chronicles of the Early Colonial Period,* ed. Rolena Adorno (Syracuse, N.Y.: Maxwell School of Citizenship and Public Affairs, 1982), presents studies of several Peruvians, including Guaman Poma, who contributed to the transition from an oral tradition to a written literature.

57. A comprehensive study of the illustrations and their significance in Guaman Poma is Mercedes López-Baralt, *Icono y conquista: Guaman Poma de Ayala* (Madrid: Hiperion, 1988).

58. *Letter to a King,* trans. Christopher Dilke, 20. Cf. *Nueva coronica,* 1:7.

59. For a discussion of the mythical aspects of the *Nueva corónica,* see Ossio, "Myth and History," 54.

60. Ibid., 88.

Chapter 6

José de Arriaga
Extirpation and Persuasion in the New World

The conception of rhetoric which emerges from the Spanish domin-ions of the sixteenth century is one divided between a classical rhetoric and an evangelical rhetoric, between a rhetoric of orating to Europeans and one of preaching to pagans, between a rhetoric of exhorting the faithful and one of converting the infidel—in short, one rhetoric intended for Europeans and another rhetoric intended for Amerindians. The di-vided nature of New World rhetoric is present in almost all the texts examined thus far. It is conspicuous in the contrast between Granada's *Ecclesiaticae rhetoricae* and his *Breve tratado* and in the distinctions be-tween Acosta's *De procuranda* and Las Casas's *De unico vocationis modo*. The rupture is evident, too, in the works of mestizos such as Valadés and Garcilaso de la Vega, in the tension between their American heri-tage and their European education.

This divided conception of rhetoric, present in the sixteenth cen-tury, becomes even more pronounced in the seventeenth. Nowhere is this widening separation between American and European, conversion and persuasion, more visible than in the career and writings of José de Arriaga. Arriaga, a teacher of rhetoric in the Jesuit colleges of Lima and an "extirpator" of idolatry in the Peruvian highlands, wrote two books that reflect these disparate aspects of his life: *Rhetoris Christiani* (1619) and *Extirpación de la idolatría en el Perú* (1621). While both books are clearly rhetorical, it is equally clear that Arriaga conceived of them as belong-ing to two entirely different projects.

José de Arriaga: Rhetor and Extirpator

Arriaga, born in Spain's Basque region in 1564, entered the Jesuit novitiate in 1579 and was educated at the Society of Jesus' *colegios* in

Ocaña and Madrid. He later taught in the colleges of Ocaña and at Vergara. In 1584 Arriaga departed for Peru, and, upon reaching Lima the following year, he was assigned to teach rhetoric at the Jesuit College of San Pablo. In 1588 Arriaga was named the first rector of the College of San Martín, a position he would hold for over twenty years. He went to Spain in 1601 to serve briefly as procurator for the Society, returning to Peru in 1603. Early in the seventeenth century Arriaga was sent to the Peruvian interior to investigate the reports of persistent idolatry among the native population. As his biographer says, Arriaga "proved to be a zealous missionary and performed his task in an admirable manner, not limiting himself to catechizing and preaching to the Indians but also carrying out profound investigations concerning the religion of the natives and bequeathing us in print the fruit of his investigations."[1] This bequest is *Extirpación de la idolatría en el Perú*, the work for which Arriaga is best known. In 1622 Arriaga was dispatched by his superior to Rome. Departing Havana harbor, the ship on which he was a passenger encountered a storm and sank. José de Arriaga died on 6 September 1622.

Arriaga's life in Peru was that of a teacher and preacher: he taught rhetoric to mostly Spanish students at San Martín and preached to the Indians in the provinces. From his arrival in Peru Arriaga was associated with the colleges of San Pablo and San Martín. San Pablo, founded in 1568 as the first Jesuit *colegio* in South America, proved to be the most durable Jesuit institution in the Spanish empire, surviving until the Society was expelled from Spanish territory in 1767.[2] The College of San Martín was founded in 1582 and shared with San Pablo the Jesuit mission of bringing humanistic education to the New World.

The Jesuit colleges in Mexico and Peru were modeled after the order's schools in Europe and, like them, were guided by the *Ratio studiorum*, the Jesuit plan of studies. The educational objectives of the *Ratio studiorum* were being developed as early as 1540, and preliminary versions were issued in 1586 and 1589. The definitive version of the *Ratio studiorum* was promulgated in 1599. The plan was itself derived from the pedagogical precepts of antiquity and, like classical education, was intended to produce students who were masters of eloquence.[3] To achieve this goal the *Ratio studiorum* stipulated that five courses were to be taken over a period of five years: three courses in progressively advanced Latin and Greek grammar, followed by a course in humanities, and culminating in the study of rhetoric. The humanities class acted as a kind of transition between the grammatical studies and rhetorical studies. Edward Lynch summarizes the content of this course:

The aim of this class is to lay the foundation for eloquence, after the
pupils have finished the grammar classes. This is done in three ways:
by a knowledge of the language, some erudition, and a sketch of the
precepts pertaining to rhetoric. For a command of the language, which
consists chiefly in acquiring propriety of expression and fluency, the
one orator used in daily prelections is Cicero; among historians, Cae-
sar, Sallust, Livy, Curtius, and others like them; among the poets, Virgil,
excepting some of the eclogues and the fourth book of the *Aeneid,* as
well as Horace's *Odes,* and elegies, epigrams, and other works of classic
poets.[4]

After completing the class in humanities, the student was ready for
the study of rhetoric, the goal of which was to attain

perfect eloquence, which comprises two great faculties, the oratorical
and the poetical. It regards not only the practical but also the cultural.
For the precepts of oratory, Cicero may be supplemented by Aristotle
and Quintilian. Style is to be formed on Cicero, though help may be
drawn from approved historians and poets. Erudition will be derived
from the history and manners of nations, and from the authorities of
writers and every sort of learning.[5]

With Arriaga's arrival in Lima the College of San Pablo was able, for
the first time in its brief life, to offer the entire curriculum required by
the *Ratio studiorum.* Arriaga's presence permitted the *colegio* to fulfill its
purpose of replicating Renaissance education in Peru. As Luis Martín
observes, "European humanists like Erasmus and Luis Vives would have
understood well the nature of the schools of humanities of colonial
Peru."[6]

The rhetoric text specified in the 1599 *Ratio studiorum* was *De arte
rhetorica libri tres, ex Aristotele, Cicerone, et Quinctiliano praecipue deprompti*
(1557?) of Cypriano Suárez, S.J. (1524–93). Although Suárez's *De arte
rhetorica* was not required until 1599, it was in use in Jesuit colleges well
before that date. Because of its association with the *Ratio studiorum, De
arte rhetorica* became one of the most widely used of all Renaissance rhetoric textbooks in Europe and, of course, in the New World as well. According to Lynch, the *Ratio studiorum* of 1599 was made mandatory in
some 245 Jesuit schools in Europe and Latin America.[7] Presumably,
Suárez's book was used in a great many of these schools. *De arte rhetorica*
was adopted as the text in rhetoric at San Pablo.[8] In Mexico portions of

Suárez's work were included in Bernardino de Llanos's *Illustrium autorum collectanea* (1604), an anthology of rhetorical and poetical texts designed for use in the society's colleges in New Spain.

Suárez's book is well suited to the Jesuit goal of *eloquentia perfecta*—it is a distillation of the precepts from the great rhetorical triumvirate of antiquity: Cicero, Aristotle, and Quintilian. As much as he admires these three authorities, Suárez believes that no single ancient text dealt adequately with the entire art of rhetoric. Suárez proceeds to enumerate the faults of each of the basic treatises written by his three sources.[9] Because of these inadequacies, Suárez says "our [Jesuit] teachers desired: to collect all the elements of eloquence in some book, method, and plan; to explain these with definitions and to illustrate them with examples from the teaching of Aristotle; in the case of Cicero and Quintilian to include not only their teaching but usually their very words."[10] This is precisely what Suárez does, with the intention of assisting "young men to read the learned books of Aristotle, Cicero, and Quintilian wherein lie the well-springs of eloquence."[11]

Suárez is committed to the utility of ancient precepts and sees no reason to tinker with them in the sixteenth century. He is aware, he says, "that many of the teachings handed down by the ancients are attacked even in published books by people who should more reasonably have defended them. However, since many persons of exceptional learning have defended these teachings, I have decided not to change, without a good reason, what the judgment of so many centuries of learning has approved. In fact, I strongly urge you, Christian reader, to uproot completely from your mind this inordinate desire to contradict ancient writers rashly, so that it does not then proceed further towards the undoing of your intellect."[12]

Having thus affirmed the superiority of ancient precepts, Suárez proceeds to present a compendium of classical rhetoric. In his introduction Suárez summarizes *De arte rhetorica* this way:

> In the first book, which concerns invention, sixteen topics for arguments are explained, and at the same time the matter suitable for arousing hearers is extracted from them. Certain rules are also set forth adapted to embellishment and deliberation [demonstrative and deliberative speaking].
>
> The second book which contains rules for arrangement treats the divisions of a speech, the *status*, judgment, and the kind of dispute which arises over the meaning of a writing. Also, syllogistic reason-

ing, enthymeme, induction, and example are treated. Besides, since ancient writers frequently refer to the epichereme, sorites, and dilemma, the effectiveness of these is explained.

Finally, the third book teaches the embellishment of speech contained in words, either simple or compound. It also discusses rare and new words, tropes, ornaments of words and of thoughts; the origin, cause, nature, and use of well knit metrical prose; and finally, it treats memory and delivery.[13]

Thus, students in Jesuit colleges could expect to be exposed to unadulterated classical rhetoric, whether in Europe or Mexico or Peru.

Although Suárez's book was available in Peru, Arriaga decided to write his own rhetoric text, *Rhetoris Christiani,* which he dedicated to the students of the College of San Martín. This book was in turn based on another Jesuit rhetoric, the *Orator Christianus* (1612) of Carlo Reggio (1540–1612).[14] Like Suárez's *De arte rhetorica,* Arriaga's *Rhetoris Christiani* is comprehensively classical in orientation. Arriaga begins with a book devoted to the nature of rhetoric, followed by books devoted to invention, disposition, elocution, memory, and pronunciation. For examples of effective rhetorical techniques Arriaga frequently invokes Cicero and Virgil. Given his throughgoing classicism and his fondness for Ciceronian oratory and Virgilian poetry, it is not surprising that one of his students at San Martín called Arriaga a "Cicero of oratory" and a "Virgil of poetry."[15] Thus, whether Arriaga was using Suárez's work or his own, he provided his students in Lima a rhetorical education faithful to the *Ratio studiorum* and, therefore, the classical tradition.

At about the same time that the *Rhetoris Christiani* was being printed in Lyons, Arriaga was at work on another book, the one for which he would become best known, *Extirpación de la idolatría en Perú.* This work, published in Lima in 1621, reflects the changing nature of the church's enterprise in the New World. The evangelization of the sixteenth century was being replaced by a religious consolidation in the seventeenth century. Sabine MacCormack contends that in the seventeenth century "Peruvian missionaries had crossed the gulf separating the enterprise of preaching the gospel of all nations from that of extirpating non-Christian religion . . . the apostolic labor of preaching and persuading was to be supplemented by the more authoritarian labor of implementing what had been preached by extirpation."[16]

This shift in missionary policy was prompted by the disturbing persistence of indigenous religious practices in Peru. Acosta, Las Casas, and many others had warned of the great difficulties and uncertainties confronting the evangelist in the New World. These warnings were confirmed when Spaniards began to discover that Christianized Andeans continued to venerate *huacas,* the sacred objects and places that had been worshiped by their ancestors. The continuation of these traditional practices was so pervasive that the presumed success of native conversions in the previous century suddenly appeared highly dubious. Thus, in the first half of the seventeen century the Spanish initiated campaigns of "extirpation," to discover and destroy the idolatry of the Andeans.

Arriaga's participation in such a campaign in 1616–17 provides the basis for the *Extirpación de la idolatría.* This book become a kind of instruction manual for those who would be extirpators and who needed detailed directions about how to proceed. Arriaga tells his reader that *Extirpación de la idolatría* may be divided into three parts: "The first: What idols and huacas the Indians have and what sacrifices and festivals they perform. What ministers and priests they have and what their abuses and superstitions in paganism are to this very day. Second: Why, since they are Christians, and even the sons and grandsons of Christians, this evil has not been uprooted, and what the means are of uprooting it. Third: How, in detail, visits for the extirpation of idolatry should be carried out."[17]

In the third and final portion of the book, in particular, Arriaga addresses the problem of preaching and promises his book will show "the preachers the truths they must teach and the errors they must refute."[18] Despite his attention to preaching, Arriaga's *Extirpación de la idolatría* differs significantly from the more evangelical approach of preaching manuals such as Las Casas's *De unico vocationis modo* or Acosta's *De procuranda.* Arriaga recommends Acosta's book to his readers but notes that the *Extirpación de la idolatría* has a different purpose.[19] Unlike his predecessors, Arriaga can assume that the native audience has been exposed to the basic tenets of Christianity. Arriaga must inform the extirpator of the methods available to compel the natives to conform to the beliefs already presented and to reject the religious customs of their ancestors.

Arriaga begins his guide for the would-be extirpator by noting that the persistence of idolatry in Peru is to be expected. In Spain the Gospel was preached "by sainted prelates and doctors and watered with the blood of famous martyrs, yet even so idolatry raised its head and could not be cut down."[20] Arriaga also reminds his readers that thus far in Peru the Gospel had been preached for only about ninety years and that it required some six hundred years for idolatry to be eradicated in Spain. Even after so many centuries, says Arriaga, certain superstitions remain in Spain. "The Jews," he says, "are outsiders there still despite the fact that they came to the country more than 1,500 years ago, in the time of the Emperor Claudius. For it has scarcely been possible to extirpate so evil a seed even in so clean a land, where the Gospel has been so continuously, so carefully, and so thoroughly preached and where the Most Righteous Tribunal of the Holy Office has been so diligently and solicitously vigilant."[21] Arriaga continues, indicating that the difficulty of correcting "errors of belief learned at a mother's breast and inherited from father to son can readily be seen in the recent example we have before us in the expulsion of the Moors from Spain. For they were provided with every possible remedy for their evils without effecting their true conversion, as intended, and, since the disease was more powerful than the medicine and there was no hope of spiritual remedy, it became necessary as with misguided folk to expel them from the country."[22] Despite these rather discouraging Spanish precedents, Arriaga is optimistic about the possibilities for purifying the New World. Compared to the Moors and the Jews of Spain "the disease of our Indians is not so deeply rooted a cancer. The remedy is easy for those who wished to be cured, as they do when their disease is pointed out to them. What is needed is a cure, or cures, and the realization that the evil is worse than was supposed."[23]

Arriaga is addressing one of the most persistent problems that confronted Spanish Catholicism: the inability to achieve the conversion of the infidels living in the Spanish empire. Despite the conviction of divine support and notwithstanding the great dedication of the clergy, frustratingly little progress had been made among unbelievers. This frustration led to extreme measures, including those Arriaga mentions: the Inquisition and the expulsions. The precedents of coercion in the face of recalcitrant infidels would not be lost on the colonial clergy. The process of extirpation was partially modeled after the Inquisition, and, like the Holy Office, the extirpators would often resort to harsh remedies.

But before those remedies could be administered the "visitors," itinerant investigators of idolatry, must have the means to discover the extent to which "the disease" had spread in the various provinces. Arriaga therefore provides information about the covert religious practices that the extirpator might be expected to encounter, detailing the *huacas*, *pacarinas*, *malquis*, and all the other objects and sites worshiped in great variety by the Andeans. Compared to the missionary treatises of the sixteenth century, Arriaga has relatively little to say about Christian doctrine. The discovery of idolatry had made it imperative that the priests understand the forces that they were opposing. Armed with such knowledge of the native superstitions, the extirpators would, of course, be in a better position to recognize such deviant practices when they were encountered. Idolatry had been permitted to flourish only because its practice had been so well hidden by the native peoples.

Arriaga credits Francisco de Avila (ca. 1573–1647) with the discovery of this surreptitious devil worship. Through preaching and investigation Avila uncovered some six hundred idols among the Indians of Huarochirí province. These idols were burned in Lima's Plaza de Armas in 1609, an event that marked the beginning of a systematic and relentless campaign of extirpation.

For the campaign against idolatry to be successful Arriaga believes it is first necessary to understand the causes of the evil. He says that the primary cause of the persistence of idolatry "is the failure to teach Christian doctrine; if this could be remedied the remaining sources and roots would dry up and disappear."[24] All too often, says Arriaga, Indians who recite Christian doctrine "do so in a parrotlike manner without any understanding of what they are saying."[25] The inability to comprehend Christianity is attributed by Arriaga to the inadequate instruction they have received. Too many priests do not know Quechua and know "still less what to preach."[26] Arriaga virtually admits that much of the missionary endeavor of the previous century was a failure. At best, a thin veneer of Christianity was laid over traditional and familial worship, resulting in an unacceptable syncretic religion. The goal of extirpation was both to deepen the Andeans' knowledge of Christianity and to remove their residual paganism.

Teaching and preaching, says Arriaga, are the basic tools available to the extirpator of idolatry. Teaching is the most important activity for a visitor to undertake, but teaching can be partially accomplished through preaching. Thus, the visitor must be an accomplished preacher and should be accompanied on the visits by monks to preach and catechize the Indians. A visit, says Arriaga, "has more to do with the heart than with the body, and more relation to industry than to force, and pertains more to mercy than to justice. Indeed, the paraphernalia and tumult of justice must be curtailed as much as can be, and Christian teaching, sermons, and confessions emphasized, so that the visitor, like the fathers that go with him, may show that he and they are in effect fathers and teachers and not crown agents or judges."[27]

Arriaga believes that, for preaching to perform its role in extirpating idolatry, it is essential to improve the quality of the sermons. To this end he suggests that local priests prepare written drafts of their sermons for inspection by the visitor prior to delivery. For the priest who is unable or unwilling to do this, says Arriaga, "let him read the Indians a printed sermon at least on Sundays and feast days."[28] "No one can do less than this," concludes Arriaga, and he clearly expects that most preachers will do more. Arriaga indicates that in his experience the most effective visits were those for which "visitors were chosen who were experienced in Indian affairs, who knew the language, and who had some skill in the pulpit. They had also to be learned men and theologians who knew how to make themselves understood and how to teach ignorant people the mysteries of our holy faith."[29]

Arriaga naturally expects that the visitors and the priests accompanying them will be capable of composing their own discourses. Such sermons should be adapted to the capacity of the native audience, "arguing with them by natural reasons that they can understand, rather than by samples of fine writing."[30] Sermons should, for the most part, expound on one theme in a simple and direct way. Arriaga stipulates the subjects for twelve sermons, beginning with the singularity of the Christian God and concluding with divine judgment, damnation, and salvation.[31] Arriaga apparently intends that all twelve of the proposed themes would be presented during a visit. He notes that the material can be condensed or amplified to fit the precise length of a given visit.

In addition to presenting basic Christian doctrine, sermons must also exhort the villagers to reveal the location of their *huacas* to the visitor.[32] Unfortunately, Arriaga had learned from experience that preaching alone rarely results in the discovery of *huacas*. While preaching is an important part of a visit, sermons are themselves insufficient to achieve extirpation. Father Avila, the "discoverer" of idolatry, found that much information about the existence of idols could be gained by the careful questioning of the Indians. Interrogation, therefore, becomes an important tool in the process of extirpation, and Arriaga includes considerable advice about how to examine suspected idolaters. While he says much about compassion and forgiveness, ultimately Arriaga believes idolatry must be dealt with harshly. An essential element of extirpation was the physical destruction of the *huacas*. Thus, Spaniards burned, buried, and smashed countless objects of traditional and familial veneration and worship to achieve the complete physical eradication of idolatry.

Just as extirpation required the eradication of the physical symbols of idolatry, so too must the indigenous priesthood be rooted out. Sorcerers, native priests, and unrepentant idolaters were to be dealt with severely. Sorcerers who resisted rehabilitation should be imprisoned. Arriaga was himself assigned the responsibility of supervising the construction of a "house of detention" near Lima for the incarceration of "sorcerers." To avoid the perpetuation of idolatry the children of native nobility must be carefully educated. Arriaga participated in the decision to establish a school for native nobility in the town of Cercado (also the location of the house of detention). This college would ensure that Christian teaching would occur far from the corrupting influence of the idolaters in the interior. Through the incarceration of sorcerers and the inculcation of children, the extirpators hoped that the evil of idolatry would be eradicated finally and forever.

The *Extirpación de la idolatría* contains little new information about the procedures and techniques of proselytizing in Peru. What is significant is the thoroughness, the relentlessness, even the desperation, of the measures which Arriaga describes and recommends. The campaign of extirpation could not help but have enormous consequences for the relationship between the Europeans and the Andeans. As a result of the extirpations, says MacCormack, "Peru became a land of two separate societies, or, as seventeenth-century jurists expressed it, 'republics,' between which little cultural exchange was possible."[33]

The widening division between the "two separate societies" of Peru is reflected in the *Extirpación de la idolatría* and the *Rhetoris Christiani*. Both were written by the same man, at about the same time; one is a work of rhetorical practice, the other of rhetorical theory. Yet, in spite of these shared attributes, the two books are quite different. Arriaga himself gives no indication that he recognizes any close bond between them. The *Extirpación de la idolatría* and the *Rhetoris Christiani* are clearly artifacts of two different worlds, the New and the Old. The *Rhetoris Christiani* is a product of the academy with little direct recognition of the circumstances of seventeenth-century Peru. Rather, it is a work dedicated to the continuation of an ancient tradition in a new location. In contrast, the *Extirpación de la idolatría* is a practical guide for immediate action. It is committed not to the continuation of old traditions but, rather, to their eradication. The *Extirpación de la idolatría* also marks the end of a debate of sorts, more implicit than explicit, about the appropriate measures for evangelization. Despite the importance he attaches to preaching, Arriaga recognizes that peaceful persuasion alone is insufficient for the task at hand. He accepts the necessity of coercive measures against native religions, including the destruction of venerated objects and the imprisonment of practitioners, if Christianity is to triumph over paganism. Peaceful persuasion, of course, had never been unreservedly endorsed by the church and its missionaries as the exclusive method of conversion. The case for persuasion as the evangelist's preferred instrument was seriously discredited by Francisco de Avila's exposure of the failures of the sixteenth-century conversions.

The disparities between the *Rhetoris Christiani* and the *Extirpación de la idolatría* reflect the evolution of rhetoric in Spain's American empire. Rhetoricians, reluctant to adapt to Mesoamerican or Andean circumstances, were generally content to perpetuate European doctrine. At the same time, conversion manuals, which presumably were adapted to New World conditions, often reflect only the barest recognition of the rhetorical tradition. It is entirely appropriate that the *Rhetoris Christiani* was published in Europe; it is a European book. The *Rhetoris Christiani* signals clearly that the rhetoric of the New World had reverted to the familiar dogma of the Old.

Rhetoric: New World and Old

Two very different, and often incompatible, conceptions of rhetoric emerged from the New World in the seventeenth century. The division of rhetoric into two different theories of persuasion—a complete and complex one for Europeans and another, compressed and simple, for Amerindians—was apparent in many of the rhetorics of the sixteenth century. Granada and Acosta, in particular, preceded Arriaga in presenting views that clearly divided rhetoric into two distinct persuasive theories determined by the presumed capacity of the audience to be addressed. Las Casas, with his expansive view of humanity, was virtually alone in insisting that the same persuasive strategies could be applied to both Indian and European audiences. Yet even Las Casas, by advocating the missionary's use of unaltered classical rhetoric, denies the possibility of persuasive approaches adapted to the cultural conditions of the Amerindians. Virtually alone, Valadés proceeds tentatively toward modifying European rhetoric for American needs in the *Rhetorica Christiana*. His remarkable incorporation of a narrative of native life into the framework of Ciceronian rhetoric demonstrates an awareness and understanding of the peoples around him. Moreover, his elevation of *memoria* and visual imagery, while derived from Renaissance sources, is also a product of his experience among the Mexica. Yet, despite these concessions to American culture, Valadés's *Rhetorica Christiana* remains very much a rhetoric in the European tradition.

The division of rhetoric into European and American variants was reinforced by the increasing retreat of rhetoric from the countryside into the academy. The rejection of an Indian and mestizo clergy by the church removed the most compelling reason to provide rhetorical training to native peoples. Consequently, the goal of teaching Indians to speak Latin like Cicero seemed less desirable and attainable than it did in the previous century. With rhetorical training reserved for Spanish and Creole students there was little need to consider anything but traditional approaches to persuasion. Rhetoric, like the educational system of which it was a part, became segregated from the larger society. Dedicated to the replication and perpetuation of European culture, the educational curriculum had little room for attention to indigenous cultures. Cloistered in European-like centers of learning, rhetoricians had no compelling incentive to understand the variety of audiences potentially available to the orator in the Americas.

The place of rhetoric in the academy was established at the very beginning of higher education in the New World and was, of course, a reflection of the centrality of rhetoric in the European curriculum. On 12 July 1553 Francisco Cervantes de Salazar initiated the university study of rhetoric in New Spain. Cervantes, the first professor of rhetoric at the Royal and Pontifical University of Mexico, wrote a series of dialogues intended to teach Latin to students in Mexico. These dialogues, together with a commentary on the *Exertatio linguae Latina* of the Spanish humanist Juan Luis Vives, were published in 1554 by Juan Pablos, New Spain's first printer.[34] In one of his dialogues Cervantes offers a description of his course: "Professor Cervantes teaches rhetoric, and he is heard by many students of the other sciences as well as those interested in oratory, because rhetoric is an equipment for these studies."[35] Unfortunately, Cervantes does not say what he told these "many students," but his reputation as a Latinist, an orator, and an ardent humanist leaves little doubt that he would have sought to introduce his students faithfully to the European rhetorical tradition.

Cervantes's successors in the universities and *colegios* of the New World labored to continue the transfer of the humanistic curriculum from

Europe to colonial institutions. Like Arriaga's *Rhetoris Christiani*, the seventeenth-century Jesuit treatises printed in America adhered to the society's commitment to classical rhetoric.[36] Bernardino de Llanos' *Illustrium autorum collectanea* (Mexico, 1604), an anthology of the major Jesuit rhetorical and poetical texts, includes portions of Suárez's *De arte rhetorica*, Pedro Juan Nuñez's *Progymnasmata* (Zaragoza, 1591), and Bartolomé Bravo's *Liber de conscribendus epistolis* (Segovia, 1591).[37] Llanos's *Illustrium autorum collectanea* presents the essential documents of the Jesuit educational system together in one volume for use in Mexico, where the individual treatises might well be difficult to obtain. In addition to Llanos's, other Jesuits in Mexico composed original rhetorical treatises. Notable among these are Tomás González's two works of 1646, one entitled, in the manner of Suárez, *De arte rhetorica libri tres* and, the other, the *Summa totius rhetoricae*.[38] Both of these works present thorough accounts of classical rhetoric organized around the five parts of Ciceronian theory.

In 1625 Domingo Velázquez wrote the *Breve instrucción, y summa rethórica de predicadores,* possibly the first rhetoric written in New Spain in Spanish, rather than in Latin. As was the case in Spain, the use of the vernacular made little initial difference in the nature of rhetorical treatises.[39] Velázquez's *Breve instrucción* is, in many respects, typical of post-Tridentine preaching manuals. Velázquez begins with a discussion of the special problems presented by the study of preaching and a brief statement on the methods of scriptural analysis. He also justifies the use of the *letras humanas* for the divine purposes of the preacher. After this justification Velázquez settles into an account of classical rhetoric adapted more or less to the needs of the preacher. The *Breve instrucción*, like the *Illustrium autorum collectanea* and the *De arte rhetorica*, is dedicated to the transference of the classical rhetoric from Europe to the New World. There is indeed little in these works of Velázquez, Llanos, or Gonzalez that would inform a reader that these books had originated anywhere other than Europe.

Ultimately, then, the story of rhetoric in the New World is the story of the continuation of the European tradition on a grand scale. It was perhaps inevitable that rhetoric in Spain's American empire would have remained so faithful to its European origins, for in the sixteenth and seventeenth centuries there were formidable barriers to achieving a true transformation of this venerable discipline. The first of these barriers was the very strength of the rhetorical tradition itself. The Renaissance was inspired by a resurgence of classical learning in which the art of rhetoric had played an important role. Renaissance writers labored long and hard to rehabilitate rhetoric from what they believed to be its medieval degradation. Having struggled to restore classical rhetoric, many Renaissance thinkers were understandably reluctant to entertain revisions that could not be sanctioned by invoking ancient authorities.

This is certainly not to suggest that the entirety of Renaissance rhetoric was simply a recapitulation of the classical inheritance. Indeed, Renaissance rhetoric is characterized by debates, often quite heated, about the nature of rhetoric and the merits of ancient authors. It may even be accurate to characterize the rhetorical innovations that occurred in the Renaissance as "revolutionary." Valla, Agricola, Ramus, Vives, and others proposed significant revisions in sixteenth-century rhetoric.[40] Ramus, in particular, attacked the Renaissance reverence for classical authorities.[41] Yet, despite all the indictments of and alterations to the rhetorical tradition by its sixteenth-century critics, the classical orientation of Renaissance rhetoric remains conspicuous. While Cicero's preeminence as a rhetorical theorist and Latin stylist was frequently challenged, the Roman orator remained a dominant and often-quoted figure. More important, ancient authorities continued to define the very nature of the debates. Thus, a fundamental and recurrent issue for Renaissance rhetoricians was the extent to which a particular theorist's work deviated from or remained faithful to classical models.

The challenges to the classical tradition presented by proponents of rhetorical innovation often had significant consequences for the development of rhetorical theory. Yet, when compared to the possibility of creating a rhetoric capable of understanding and guiding communication with the natives of the New World, European debates about the nature of rhetoric can appear to be disputations of the most arcane kind. The controversies over the relationship between rhetoric and dialectic, the proper placement of topical invention, or the appropriate extent of Ciceronianism were sufficiently compelling that European theorists were unable or unwilling to attend to the rhetorical consequences of the Columbian encounter. Even the most innovative of European rhetorical theorists rarely display any awareness of the possibilities presented by the New World. By remaining rooted in Europe, the Renaissance efforts to rehabilitate rhetoric may have lost the opportunity to truly "revolutionize" rhetoric in the sixteenth century.

With the exception of writers such as Granada, who have an immediate interest in the conversion enterprise, even Spanish rhetoricians
manifest little concern for the rhetorical potentialities presented by the
colonization of America. Just as the persistence of the rhetorical tradition would inhibit rhetorical innovation, the desire to convert native
peoples would, rather ironically, inhibit the adaptation of rhetoric to
American circumstances. The role of rhetoric in the New World was, of
course, typically justified as an instrument of Christianization. Nevertheless, the desire to achieve a total and lasting conversion led to an
impatience with rhetorical methods that were, by their very nature, incremental. The exasperation of both the church and the crown with the
inability to achieve extensive and permanent conversions among the
Jewish and Muslim populations resulted in the expulsions of these
groups from Spain. It was, of course, not feasible to expel the peoples of
the New World from their own lands. (The Spanish did, however, engage in *reducción,* a program of forced resettlement of native peoples
into new villages, where they could be better controlled.) The Spanish
attempts to Christianize the Jewish and Islamic communities yielded
few, if any, strategies that could be employed by the missionaries in the
New World. On the contrary, Spanish experience with the recalcitrance
of nonbelievers established the precedent for favoring coercion over
persuasion. The campaign of extirpation was, like the peninsular expulsions, born of Spanish frustration with the inexplicable intractability of
infidels and pagans.

The impatience with extensive reliance on rhetorical methods was
intensified by the Protestant Reformation and the Catholic response. The
earliest colonization in Mexico and Peru had taken place during a period in Spain of comparative enlightenment and receptiveness to
Erasmian humanism and other potentially heterodox movements. This
climate made possible a certain amount of experimentation in the conversion of the natives of the New World.[42] With the defection of Germany and England to the Protestant apostasy, the earlier tolerance was
replaced with a renewed religious zeal. Thus, it appeared that the New
World's peoples had been delivered to Spain for conversion to Catholicism in compensation for those Europeans lost to Protestantism. A conversion campaign driven by a conviction of infallibility and an urgency
of action could have little tolerance for incremental persuasion by rhetorical means.

Eventually, and perhaps inevitably, the strength of the rhetorical tradition and the fervor of religious intolerance combined to inhibit rhetoric from adapting fully to the exigencies presented by the New World. These constraints, however, did not mean that the course of rhetoric in Mexico and Peru was uneventful, any more than the persistence of classical norms meant that Renaissance rhetoric was unimaginative or unoriginal. Indeed, the story of rhetoric in the New World is that of a grand experiment in which rhetoricians attempted to accomplish that which was unimaginable, indeed impossible, before 1492. Never before had Europeans attempted to record and preserve the discourse of an indigenous people as did Sahagún and his native assistant as they transcribed the ancient word for his *General History*. Never before had a person born in America written a rhetoric, much less included in such a treatise an account of native customs, as did Valadés in the *Rhetorica Christiana*. Never before had Europeans so generously praised the eloquence of non-Europeans, as did Sahagún, Valadés, and Garcilaso. Never before had anyone attempted to apply faithfully the principles of classical rhetoric to a New World audience as did Las Casas in *De unico vocationis modo*. And never before had subjugated peoples so skillfully directed the rhetorical techniques in an effort to alter European colonial policy as did Guaman Poma in the *Nueva corónica* and Garcilaso in the *Royal Commentaries*.

The rhetoricians whose works were written in or inspired by the New World all, in differing degree, address the fundamental problem of how people of different languages, cultures, religions, indeed different worlds, can communicate meaningfully with one another. They did not arrive at completely satisfactory solutions to this problem, but, then, cultural divisions have proven to be persistent barriers to human cooperation. The works of Sahagún, Valadés, Las Casas, and others represent the beginnings of an inquiry into the possibility of communication between cultures. The subsequent centuries have demonstrated dramatically just how elusive peaceful persuasion between different peoples can be. The rhetoricians of New Spain and Peru, facing situations unimagined by Aristotle or Cicero, nevertheless looked for inspiration to their Greek and Roman predecessors. The rhetorical tradition was too venerable and the Christian mission too righteous to permit the development of a rhetoric that deviated significantly from European norms. Thus, rhetoric, one of the great intellectual achievements of Europe, was transported to the New World while remaining faithful to the traditions of the Old.

Notes

1. Carlos A. Romero, "Father Pablo José de Arriaga," in *The Extirpation of Idolatry in Peru*, by Pablo Joseph de Arriaga, trans. L. Clark Keating (Lexington: University of Kentucky Press, 1968), xviii.

2. For a history of this institution, see Luis Martín, *The Intellectual Conquest of Peru: The Jesuit College of San Pablo, 1568–1767* (New York: Fordham University Press, 1968).

3. For an extensive discussion of the place of rhetoric in Jesuit education, see Edward Lynch, S.J., "The Origin and Development of Rhetoric in the Plan of Studies of 1599 of the Society of Jesus" (Ph.D. diss., Northwestern University, 1968). See also François de Dainville, *L'Education des jésuites* (Paris: Minuit, 1978), esp. chap. 2, "Humanites classiques," 167–307.

4. Lynch, "Origin and Development," 261.

5. Ibid., 262.

6. *The Kingdom of the Sun* (New York: Scribner's, 1974), 96.

7. Lynch, "Origin and Development," 258.

8. Martín, *Intellectual Conquest*, 40.

9. *The* De Arte Rhetorica *(1568) by Cyprian Soarez, S.J.: A Translation with Introduction and Notes*, Lawrence J. Flynn, S.J. (Ph.D. diss., University of Florida, 1955), 105–7.

10. Ibid., 108.

11. Ibid.

12. Ibid., 108–9.

13. Ibid., "Introduction II," 112–13.

14. For a discussion of Reggio's work, see Marc Fumarolli, *L'Age de l'éloquence: Rhétorique et "res literaria" de la Renaissance au seuil de l'époque classique* (Paris: Albin Michel, 1994), 186–90.

15. Buenaventura de Salinas y Cordova, *Memorial de las Historias del Nvevo Mvndo Pirv* [1630] (Lima: University of San Marcos, 1957), 242–43.

16. *Religion in the Andes: Vision and Imagination in Early Colonial Peru* (Princeton: Princeton University Press, 1991), 388.

17. *Extirpation*, 6.

18. Ibid.

19. Ibid., 135.

20. Ibid., 7

21. Ibid., 9.

22. Ibid. Arriaga is referring to the expulsions of the *moriscos* ordered by Philip III beginning in 1609. As Stanley Payne concludes: "expulsion of the Moriscos was the last great step in eradicating the religio-ethnic pluralism of medieval Hispania. By 1614, the unitary Catholic society had been achieved" (*A History of Spain and Portugal* [Madison: University of Wisconsin Press, 1973], 1:288).

23. *Extirpation,* 9.

24. Ibid., 60.

25. Ibid., 61.

26. Ibid., 62.

27. Ibid., 104–5.

28. Ibid., 91.

29. Ibid., 103.

30. Ibid., 109.

31. Ibid., 109–11.

32. Ibid., 113.

33. *Religion in the Andes,* 386.

34. *Commentaria in Ludovico Vives, exercitationes linguae latinae a Francisco de Cervantes de Salazar.* Cervantes' dialogues, without the commentary on Vives, have been translated into English by Minnie Lee Barrett Shepard (*Life in the Imperial and Loyal City of Mexico* [Austin: University of Texas Press, 1953]). For a discussion of Cervantes' career in Mexico, as well as his admiration for Vives, see Barrett's introduction, 1–20.

35. Ibid., 24.

36. For an account of the Jesuit's dissemination of classical education in Mexico, see Ignacio Osorio Romero, *Colegios y profesores jesuitas que enseñaron Latín en Nueva España (1572–1767)* (Mexico City: Universidad Nacional Autónoma de México, 1979). The same author's *Floresta de gramática, poética y retórica en Nueva España (1521–1767)* (Mexico City: Universidad Autonóma de México, 1980) is invaluable for the study of rhetoric in colonial Mexico.

37. My account of Llanos's work, which I have not seen, relies upon Osorio Romero, *Floresta,* 145–55.

38. These works are so similar that Osorio Romero concludes that the *Summa* is a précis of the *De arte rhetorica.* For a comparison of the two works, see *Floresta,* 227–28.

39. The first Spanish rhetoric written in Castilian is Miguel de Salinas's *Retórica en lengua castellana* (1541), which, with the exception of composition in the vernacular, is a rather conventional treatise. This work is reprinted in *La retórica en España,* ed. Elena Casas (Madrid: Editora Nacional, 1980), 39–200.

40. For a consideration of the revolutionary nature of the Renaissance restructuring of rhetoric, see Marc Cogan, "Rodolphus Agricola and the Semantic Revolutions of the History of Invention," *Rhetorica* 2 (1984): 163–94. A recent comprehensive discussion of this complex subject is Peter Mack, *Renaissance Argument: Valla and Agricola in the Traditions of Rhetoric and Dialectic* (Leiden: Brill, 1993). Peter Ramus is the most completely studied of the many reformers of rhetoric. The standard study remains Walter Ong, *Ramus, Method, and the Decay of Dialogue* (Cambridge: Harvard University Press, 1958).

41. Peter Ramus, *Arguments in Rhetoric against Quintilian,* ed. James J. Murphy and trans. Carole Newlands (DeKalb: Northern Illinois University Press, 1986);

Peter Ramus's Attack on Cicero, ed. James J. Murphy, trans. Carole Newlands (Davis, Calif.: Hermagoras Press, 1992).

42. The standard treatment of Spanish Erasmianism is Marcel Bataillon, *Erasmo y España,* trans. Antonio Alatorre (Mexico City: Fondo de Cultura Económica, 1950).

Bibliography

Abbott, Don Paul. "The Ancient Word: Rhetoric in Aztec Culture." *Rhetorica* 5 (1987): 251–64.

———. "Aztecs and Orators: Rhetoric in New Spain." *Texte* 8–9 (1989): 353–65.

———. "Juan Luis Vives: Tradition and Innovation in Renaissance Rhetoric." *Central States Speech Journal* 37 (1986): 193–203.

———. "The Renaissance." In *The Present State of Scholarship in Historical and Contemporary Rhetoric.* Ed. Winifred Bryan Horner, 84–113. Rev. ed. Columbia: University of Missouri Press, 1990.

———. "Rhetoric and Writing in Renaissance Europe and England." In *A Short History of Writing Instruction: From Ancient Greece to Modern America.* Ed. James J. Murphy, 95–120. Davis, Calif.: Hermagoras Press, 1990.

Acosta, José de. *Historia natural y moral de las Indias, en que se tratan de las cosas notables del cielo, elementos, metales plantas y animales dellas y los rotos y ceremonias, leyes y gobierno de los Indios.* Mexico City: Fondo de Cultura Económica, 1962.

———. *Obras.* Ed. Francisco Mateos. *Biblioteca de autores españoles.* Vol. 73. Madrid: Atlas, 1954.

———. *De procuranda indorum salute.* Ed. Luciano Pereña et al. *Corpus Hispanorum de Pace.* Vol. 23. Madrid: Consejo Superior de Investigaciones Científicas, 1984.

———. *Tercero catecismo y exposicion de la doctrina christiana por sermones.* In *Doctrina Christiana y catecismo para instruccion de indios.* Ed. Luciano Pereña. *Corpus Hispanorum de Pace,* 26–2:333–754. Madrid: Consejo Superior de Investigaciones Científicas, 1985.

Ad C. Herennium: De ratione dicendi (Rhetorica ad Herennium). Trans. Harry Caplan. Cambridge: Harvard University Press, 1954.

Adorno, Rolena. *Cronista y príncipe: La obra de don Felipe Guaman Poma de Ayala.* Lima: Pontifical Catholic University of Peru, 1989.

———. *Guaman Poma: Writing and Resistance in Colonial Peru.* Austin: University of Texas Press, 1986.

———, ed. *From Oral to Written Expression: Native Andean Chronicles of the Early Colonial Period.* Syracuse, N.Y.: Maxwell School of Citizenship and Public Affairs, 1982.

Aristotle. *On Rhetoric: A Theory of Civic Discourse.* Trans. George A. Kennedy. New York: Oxford University Press, 1991.

Artaza, Elena. *El ars narrandi en el siglo XVI español. Teoría y práctica.* Duesto: University of Duesto, 1989.

Arriaga, Pablo José de, S.J. *The Extirpation of Idolatry in Peru.* Ed. and trans. L. Clark Keating. Lexington: University of Kentucky Press, 1968.

————. *Rhetoris Christiani partes septem, exemplis oum sacris, tum philosophicis illustratae.* Lyon, 1619.

Augustine, Aurelius. *The First Catecetical Instruction [De Catechezandis Rudibus].* Trans. Joseph P. Christopher. Westminster, Md.: Newman Press, 1962.

Barnes-Karol, Gwendolyn. "Religious Oratory in a Culture of Control." In *Culture and Control in Counter-Reformation Spain.* Ed. Anne J. Cruz and Mary Elizabeth Perry, 51–77. Minneapolis: University of Minnesota Press, 1992.

Barranechea, Raúl Porras. *El Inca Garcilaso en Montilla.* Lima: Editorial San Marcos, 1955.

Barth, Pius J. "Franciscan Education and the Social Order in Spanish North America (1502–1821)." Ph.D. diss., University of Chicago, 1945.

Bataillon, Marcel. *Erasmo y España: estudios sobre la historia espiritual del siglo xvi.* Trans. Antonio Alatorre. Mexico City: Fondo de Cultura Económica, 1950.

Bautista, Juan. *Huehuetlahtolli.* In *Colección de documentos para la historia mexicana,* vol. 3. Ed. Antonio Peñafiel. Mexico City: Secretaría de Fomento, 1901.

Blythin, Evan. *Huei Tlatoani: The Mexican Speaker.* Lanham, Md.: University Press of America, 1990.

Burke, Kenneth. *A Rhetoric of Motives.* Berkeley: University of California Press, 1969.

Carochi, Horacio. *Arte de la lengua mexicana: con la de la declaración de los adverbios della: edición facsimilar de la publicada por Juan Ruyz en la Cuidad de Mexico, 1645.* Intro. Miguel León-Portilla. Mexico City: Universidad Nacional Autónoma de México, 1983.

Casas, Elena, ed. *La retórica en España.* Madrid: Editora Nacional, 1980.

Castro, Francisco de. *De arte rhetorica dialogi quatour.* Cordoba, 1611.

Cervantes de Salazar, Francisco. *Life in the Imperial and Loyal City of Mexico in New Spain.* Trans. Minnie Lee Barrett Shepard. Austin: University of Texas Press, 1953.

Chejne, Anwar. *Islam and the West: The Moriscos.* Albany: State University of New York Press, 1983.

Cicero, Marcus Tullius. *De inventione.* Trans. H. M. Hubbell. Cambridge: Harvard University Press, 1968.

————. *De oratore.* Trans. E. W. Sutton and Horace Rackham. 2 vols. Cambridge: Harvard University Press, 1942.

Clavijero, Francisco Javier. *Historia antigua de México.* 2 vols. Mexico City: Editorial Porrúa, 1958.

Clendinnen, Inga. *Aztecs: An Interpretation.* Cambridge: Cambridge University Press, 1991.

Cogan, Marc. "Rudolphus Agricola and the Semantic Revolutions of the History of Invention." *Rhetorica* 2 (1984): 163–94.

Conley, Thomas M. *Rhetoric in the European Tradition.* New York: Longman, 1990.

Cruz, Anne J., and Mary Elizabeth Perry, eds. *Culture and Control in Counter-Reformation Spain.* Minneapolis: University of Minnesota Press, 1992.

Dainville, François de. *L'Education des jésuites.* Paris: Minuit, 1978.

Dibble, Charles E. "The Nahuatlization of Christianity." In *Sixteenth-Century Mexico: The Work of Sahagún.* Ed. Munro S. Edmonson, 225–33. Albuquerque: University of New Mexico Press, 1974.

Dolce, Ludovico. *Dialogo nel quale si ragiona del modo di accrescere et conservar la memoria.* Venice, 1521.

D'Olwer. Luis Nicholas. *Fray Bernardino de Sahagún.* Mexico City: Instituto Panamericano de Geografía e Historia, 1952.

Duran, Juan Guillermo. *El catecismo del III concilio provincial de Lima y sus complementos pastorales (1584–1585).* Buenos Aires: Editorial El Derecho, 1982.

Edmonson, Munro S., ed. *Sixteenth-Century Mexico: The Work of Sahagún.* Albuquerque: University of New Mexico Press, 1974.

Friede, Juan, and Benjamin Keen, eds. *Bartolomé de las Casas in History: Toward an Understanding of the Man and His Work.* DeKalb: Northern Illinois University Press, 1971.

Fumaroli, Marc. *L'Age de l'éloquence: Rhétorique et "res literaria" de la Renaissance au seuil de l'époque classique.* Paris: Albin Michel, 1994.

Garcilaso de la Vega, El Inca. *The Florida of the Inca.* Ed. and trans. John Grier Varner and Jeanette Johnson Varner. Austin: University of Texas Press, 1951.

———. *Royal Commentaries of the Incas and General History of Peru.* Trans. Harold V. Livermore. 2 pts. Austin: University of Texas Press, 1966.

Garibay K., Angel Maria. *Historia de la literatura Nahuatl.* 2 vols. Mexico City: Editorial Porrúa, 1953.

George, Edward V. "Rhetoric in Vives." *Opera omnia: Ioannis Lodovici Vives,* 114–77. Valencia, 1992.

———. *Llave de Nahuatl.* Mexico City: Editorial Porrúa, 1961.

González, Tomás. *De arte rhetorica libri tres.* Mexico, 1646.

———. *Svmma totivs rhetoricae.* Mexico, 1646.

Granada, Luis de. *Obras de Fray Luis de Granada.* 3 vols. *Biblioteca de los autores españoles.* Vols. 6, 8, and 11. Madrid: Atlas, 1945.

Gray, Hanna. "Renaissance Humanism: The Pursuit of Eloquence." In *Renaissance Essays from the Journal of the History of Ideas.* Ed. Paul O. Kristeller and Philip P. Weiner, 199–216. New York: Harper, 1968.

Guaman Poma de Ayala, Felipe. *El primer nueva corónica y buen gobierno.* Ed. John V. Murra and Rolena Adorno. 3 vols. Mexico City: Siglo XXI, 1980.

———. *Letter to a King: A Peruvian King's Account of Life under the Incas and under Spanish Rule.* Ed. and trans. Christopher Dilke. New York: Dutton, 1978.

Hanke, Lewis. *Aristotle and the American Indians: A Study in Race Prejudice in the Modern World.* London: Hollis and Carter, 1959.

Hardison, O. B., Jr. *The Enduring Monument: A Study of the Idea of Praise in Renaissance Literary Theory and Practice*. Chapel Hill: University of North Carolina Press, 1962.

Huehuehtlahtolli: Testimonios de la Antigua Palabra. Intro. Miguel Léon-Portilla. Trans. Librado Silva Galeana. Mexico City: Secretaría de Educación Pública, 1991.

Heath, Shirley Brice. *Telling Tongues: Language Policy in Mexico—Colony to Nation*. New York: Columbia University Teacher's College Press, 1972.

Huerga, Alvaro. *Fray Luis de Granada: Una vida al servicio de la iglesia*. Madrid: Biblioteca de Autores Cristianos, 1988.

Isocrates. *Isocrates*. 4 vols. Trans. George Norlin. Loeb Classical Library. Cambridge: Harvard University Press, 1962.

Jara, René, and Nicholas Spadaccini, eds. *1492–1992: Re/Discovering Colonial Writing*. Minneapolis: University of Minnesota Press, 1989.

Kamen, Henry. "The Expulsion: Purpose and Consequence." In *Spain and the Jews: The Sephardi Experience 1492 and After*. Ed. Elie Kedouri, 74–91. London: Thames and Hudson, 1992.

Kartunnen, Frances, and James Lockhart, eds. *The Art of Nahuatl Speech: The Bancroft Dialogues*. Los Angeles: UCLA Latin American Center, 1987.

Kennedy, George A. *Classical Rhetoric and Its Christian and Secular Tradition from Ancient to Modern Times*. Chapel Hill: University of North Carolina Press, 1980.

Klor de Alva, Jorge. "Language, Politics, and Translation: Colonial Discourse and Classical Nahuatl in New Spain." In *The Art of Translation*. Ed Rosanna Warren, 143–62. Boston: Northeastern University Press, 1989.

———."Sahagún and the Birth of Modern Ethnography: Representing, Confessing, and Inscribing the Native Other." In *The Work of Bernardino de Sahagún: Pioneer Ethnographer of Sixteenth-Century Aztec Mexico*. Ed. J. Jorge Klor de Alva, H. B. Nicholson, and Eloise Quiñones Kleber, 31–52. Albany: Institute for Mesoamerican Studies, 1988.

Klor de Alva, J. Jorge, H. B. Nicholson, and Eloise Quiñones Kleber, eds. *The Work of Sahagún: Pioneer Ethnographer of Sixteenth-Century Aztec Mexico*. Albany: Institute for Mesoamerican Studies, 1988.

Las Casas, Bartolomé de. *In Defense of the Indians*. Ed. and trans. Stafford Poole, C.M. DeKalb: Northern Illinois University Press, 1992.

———. *Del único modo de atraer a todos los pueblos a la verdadera religión*. Trans. Augustín Millares Carlo. Mexico City: Fondo de Cultura Económica, 1942.

Leonard, Irving. "Don Quijote and the Book Trade in Lima, 1616." *Hispanic Review* 8 (1940): 285–304.

———. "On the Cuzco Book Trade, 1606." *Hispanic Review* 9 (1941): 359–75.

———. "Best Sellers of the Lima Book Trade." *Hispanic American Historical Review* 22 (1942): 5–33.

León-Portilla, Miguel. *Aztec Image of Self and Society*. Ed. Jorge Klor de Alva. Salt Lake City: University of Utah Press, 1992.

————. "Have We Really Translated the Mesoamerican 'Ancient Word'?" In *On the Translation of Native American Literatures*. Ed. Brian Swann, 313–38. Washington, D.C.: Smithsonian Institution Press, 1992.

Llaneza, Maximino. *Bibliografía del V. P. M. Fr. Luis de Granada*. 4 vols. Salamanca: Calatrava, 1926.

López Austin, Alfredo. "The Research Methods of Fray Bernardino de Sahagún: The Questionnaires." In *Sixteenth-Century Mexico*. Ed Munro S. Edmonson, 111–49. Albuquerque: University of New Mexico Press, 1974.

López-Baralt, Mercedes. *Icono y conquista: Guaman Poma de Ayala*. Madrid: Hiperion, 1988.

López Grigera, Luisa. "An Introduction to the Study of Rhetoric in 16th Century Spain." *Dispositio* 8 (1983): 1–64.

Losada, Angel. "The Controversy between Sepúlveda and Las Casas in the Junta of Valladolid." In *Bartolomé de Las Casas in History*. Ed. Juan Friede and Benjamin Keen, 279–308. DeKalb: Northern Illinois University Press, 1971.

Lynch, Edward, S.J. "The Origin and Development of Rhetoric in the Plan of Studies of 1599 of the Society of Jesus." Ph.D. diss., Northwestern University, 1968.

MacCormack, Sabine. *Religion in the Andes: Vision and Imagination in Early Colonial Peru*. Princeton: Princeton University Press, 1991.

Mack, Peter. *Renaissance Argument: Valla and Agricola in the Traditions of Rhetoric and Dialectic*. Leiden: Brill, 1993.

Marcus, Raymond. "Las Casas: A Selective Bibliography." In *Bartolomé de las Casas in History*. Ed. Juan Friede and Benjamin Keen, 603–16. DeKalb: Northern Illinois University Press, 1971.

Martí, Antonio. *La preceptiva retórica en el Siglo de Oro*. Madrid: Editorial Gredos, 1972.

Martín, Luis. *The Intellectual Conquest of Peru: The Jesuit College of San Pablo, 1568–1767*. New York: Fordham University Press, 1968.

————. *The Kingdom of the Sun: A Short History of Peru*. New York: Scribner's, 1974.

Martínez, Manuel. "Las Casas on the Conquest of America." In *Bartolomé de las Casas in History*. Ed. Juan Friede and Benjamin Keen, 309–49. DeKalb: Northern Illinois Press, 1971.

Maza, Francisco de la. "Fray Diego Valadés, escritor y grabador franciscano del siglo XVI." *Anales del Instituto de Investigaciones Estéticas* 3 (1945): 15–44.

Maxwell, Judith M., and Craig A. Hansen. *Of the Manners of Speaking the Old Ones Had: The Metaphors of Andrés de Olmos in the TULAL Manuscript*. Salt Lake City: University of Utah Press, 1992.

McAndrew, John. *The Open Air Churches of Sixteenth-Century Mexico: Atrios, Posas, Open Chapels, and Other Studies*. Cambridge: Harvard University Press, 1965.

Mignolo, Walter D. "Literacy and Colonization: The New World Experience." In *1492–1992: Re/Discovering Colonial Writing*. Ed. René Jara and Nicholas Spadaccini, 51–96. Minneapolis: University of Minnesota Press, 1989.

Monfasani, John. "Rhetoric and Humanism." In *Renaissance Humanism: Foundation, Forms, and Legacy.* Vol. 3, *Humanism and the Disciplines.* Ed. Albert Rabil Jr., 171–235. Philadelphia: University of Pennsylvania Press, 1988.

Murphy, James J., ed. *Medieval Eloquence: Studies in the Theory and Practice of Medieval Rhetoric.* Berkeley: University of California Press, 1978.

———. *Rhetoric in the Middle Ages: A History of Rhetorical Theory from St. Augustine to the Renaissance.* Berkeley: University of California Press, 1974.

———, ed. *Renaissance Eloquence: Studies in the Theory and Practice of Renaissance Rhetoric.* Berkeley: University of California Press, 1983.

———, ed. *Renaissance Rhetoric: A Short Title Catalogue.* New York: Garland, 1981.

Nebrija, Antonio de. *Grámatica en la lengua castellana.* Ed. Antonio Quilis. Madrid: Editora Nacional, 1980.

Oliver, Robert T. *Communication and Culture in Ancient India and China.* Syracuse, N.Y.: Syracuse University Press, 1971.

O'Malley, John W. *Praise and Blame in Renaissance Rome.* Durham: Duke University Press, 1979.

Ong, Walter. *Ramus, Method, and the Decay of Dialogue.* Cambridge: Harvard University Press, 1958.

———. "Tudor Writings on Rhetoric, Poetic, and Literary Theory." *Rhetoric, Romance, and Technology: Studies in the Interaction of Expression and Culture,* 48–103. Ithaca: Cornell University Press, 1971.

Oré, Luis Jerónimo de. *Symbolo Catholico Indiano, en el Qual se Declaran los Mysterios de la Fe en los tres Symbolos Catholicos, Apostolico, Niceno, y de S. Athanasio. Contine assi mesmo una Descripcion del nueve orbe, y de los naturales del. Y un orden de enseñarles la doctrina Christiana en las dos lenguas Generales Quichua Y Aymara, con un Confessionario breve y Catchismo de la Communion.* Lima, 1598.

Osorio Romero, Ignacio. *Colegios y professores jesuitas que enseñaron Latín en Nueva España (1572–1767).* Mexico City: Universidad Nacional Autónoma de México, 1979.

———. *Floresta de gramática, poética, y retórica en Nueva España (1521–1767).* Mexico City: Universidad Autónoma de México, 1980.

Ossio, Juan. "Myth and History: The Seventeenth-Century Chronicle of Guaman Poma de Ayala." In *Text in Context: The Social Anthropology of Tradition.* Ed. Ravinda K. Jain, 51–93. Philadelphia: Institute for the Study of Human Issues, 1977.

Pagden, Anthony. *The Fall of Natural Man: The American Indian and the Origins of Comparative Ethnology.* Cambridge: Cambridge University Press, 1982.

Payne, Stanley. *A History of Spain and Portugal.* 2 vols. Madison: University of Wisconsin Press, 1973.

Plato. *Phaedrus.* Trans. Harold North Fowler. Loeb Classical Library. Cambridge: Harvard University Press, 1914.

Publicius, Jacobus. *Oratoriae artis epitome.* Venice, 1482.

Quintilian. *Institutio oratoria.* Trans. H. E. Butler. 4 vols. Cambridge: Harvard University Press, 1980.

Ramus, Peter. *Arguments in Rhetoric against Quintilian*. Ed. James J. Murphy. Trans. Carole Newlands. DeKalb: Northern Illinois University Press, 1986.

―――. *Peter Ramus's Attack on Cicero*. Ed. James J. Murphy. Trans. Carole Newlands. Davis, Calif.: Hermagoras Press, 1992.

Reggio, Carlo. *Orator christianus, in quo primu[m] de consio[n]atore ipso, tum de concione, demum de concionantis . . . agitur*. Cologne, 1613.

Remesal, Antonio de, O.P. *Historia general de las Indias Occidentales y particular de la Gobernación de Chiapa Guatemala*. Ed. P. Carmelo Saenz de Santa Maria, S.J. *Biblioteca de autores españoles*. Vol. 175. Madrid: Atlas, 1964.

Ricard, Robert. *The Spiritual Conquest of Mexico: An Essay on the Apostolate and the Evangelizing methods of the Mendicant Orders of New Spain, 1523–1572*. Trans. Lesley Bird Simpson. Berkeley: University of California Press, 1966.

Rico Verdu, José. *La retórica española de los siglos XVI y XVII*. Madrid: Consejo Superior de Investigaciones Científicas, 1973.

Romberch, Johannes. *Congestorium artificiosa memorie*. Venice, 1520.

Romero, Carlos A. "Father Pablo José de Arriaga." In *The Extirpation of Idolatry in Peru*, by Pablo Joseph de Arriaga, xvii–xxiv. Trans. L. Clark Keating. Lexington: University of Kentucky Press, 1968.

Sahagún, Bernardino de. *Florentine Codex: General History of the Things of New Spain*. Trans. Arthur J. O. Anderson and Charles Dibble. 12 pts. Santa Fe, N.M.: School of American Research and University of Utah, 1950–69.

―――. *Historia general de las cosas de Nueva España*. Ed. Angel Maria Garibay K. 5 vols. Mexico City: Editorial Porrúa, 1956.

Saintsbury, George. *A History of Criticism and Literary Taste in Europe*. Edinburgh: Blackwood, 1902.

Salinas, Miguel de. *Retórica en lengua castellana*. In *La retórica en España*. Ed. Elena Casas, 39–200. Madrid: Editora Nacional, 1980.

Salinas y Cordova, Buenaventura de. *Memorial de las Historias del Nuevo Mundo Pirú*. Lima: University of San Marcos, 1957.

Scott, Izora. *Controversies over the Imitation of Cicero as a Model for Style and Some Phases of Their Influence on the Schools of the Renaissance*. New York: Teachers College, Columbia University, 1910.

Seigel, Jerrold. *Rhetoric and Philosophy in Renaissance Humanism: The Union of Eloquence and Wisdom, Petrarch to Valla*. Princeton: Princeton University Press, 1968.

Shuger, Debra. *Sacred Rhetoric: The Christian Grand Style in the English Renaissance*. Princeton: Princeton University Press, 1988.

Smith, Hilary Dansey. *Preaching in the Spanish Golden Age: A Study of Some Preachers of the Reign of Philip III*. Oxford: Oxford University Press, 1978.

Soarez, Cyprian. *The "De Arte Rhetorica" (1568) by Cyprian Soarez, S.J.: A Translation with Introduction and Notes*. Trans. Lawrence J. Flynn, S.J. Ph. D. diss., University of Florida, 1955.

Steck, Francis Borgia, O.F.M. *El primer colegio de América: Santa Cruz de Tlalteloco*. Mexico City: Centro de Estudios Franciscanos, 1944.

Struever, Nancy S. *The Language of History in the Renaissance: Rhetoric and Historical Consciousness in Florentine Humanism*. Princeton: Princeton University Press, 1970.

Sullivan, Thelma. "The Oratorical Orations, or *Huehuetlatholli*, Collected by Sahagún." In *Sixteenth-Century Mexico: The Work of Sagahún*. Ed. Munro S. Edmonson, 79–109. Albuquerque: University of New Mexico Press, 1974.

Swann, Brian, ed. *On the Translation of Native American Literatures*. Washington, D.C.: Smithsonian Institution Press, 1992.

Switzer, Rebecca. *The Ciceronian Style in Fr. Luis De Granada*. New York: Instituto de España, 1927.

Tibesar, Antonine, O.F.M. *Franciscan Beginnings in Colonial Peru*. Washington, D.C.: Academy of American Franciscan History, 1953.

Todorov, Tzvetan. *The Conquest of America: The Question of the Other*. Trans. Richard Howard. New York: Harper, 1984.

Torquemada, Juan de. *Monarquia indiana*. Ed. Miguel León-Portilla. 3 vols. Mexico City: Editorial Porrúa, 1969.

Valadés, Diego. *Retórica cristiana*. Intro. Esteban J. Palomera. Trans. Tarsicio Herrera et al. Mexico City: Universidad Nacional Autónoma de México; Fondo de Cultura Económica, 1989.

———. *Rhetorica Christiana: ad concionandi et vsvm accommodata, vtrivsq facvltatis exemplis svo loco insertis; qvae qvidem ex Indorum maxime deprompta svnt historiis. Vnde praeterdoctrinam, svma qvoqve . . . delectatio comparabitur*. Perugia, 1579.

Varner, John. *El Inca: The Life and Times of Garcilaso de la Vega*. Austin: University of Texas Press, 1968.

Velázquez, Domingo. *Breve instrucción, y summa rethórica de predicadores, para el estudio de las materias que se tratan en los sermones, y su ampliación, y disposición*. Mexico, 1628.

Vickers, Brian. "Epideictic and Epic in the Renaissance." *New Literary History* 14 (1982): 497–537.

———. *In Defence of Rhetoric*. Oxford: Oxford University Press, 1990.

Vives, Juan Luis. *Obras completas*. Trans. Lorenzo Riber. 2 vols. Madrid: Aguilar, 1944–48.

Wagner, Henry, and Helen Parrish. *The Life and Writings of Bartolomé de las Casas*. Albuquerque: University of New Mexico Press, 1967.

Ward, John O. "From Antiquity to the Renaissance: Glosses and Commentaries on Cicero's *Rhetorica*." In *Medieval Eloquence: Studies in the Theory and Practice of Medieval Rhetoric*. Ed. James J. Murphy, 25–67. Berkeley: University of California Press, 1978.

———. "Renaissance Commentators on Ciceronian Rhetoric." In *Renaissance Eloquence: Studies in the Theory and Practice of Renaissance Rhetoric*. Ed. James J. Murphy, 126–73. Berkeley: University of California Press, 1983.

Warren, Rosanna, ed. *The Art of Translation: Voices from the Field*. Boston: Northeastern University Press, 1989.

Wilkerson, S. Jeffrey K. "The Ethnographic Work of Andrés de Olmos, Precursor and Contemporary of Sahagún." In *Sixteenth Century Mexico: The Work of Sahagún*. Ed. Munro S. Edmonson, 27–77. Albuquerque: University of New Mexico Press, 1974.

Yates, Francis. *The Art of Memory*. Chicago: University of Chicago Press, 1966.

Zamora, Margarita. *Language, Authority, and Indigenous History in the* Comentarios reales de los incas. Cambridge: Cambridge University Press, 1988.

Zurita, Alonso de. *Brief and Summary Relation of the Lords of New Spain*. Ed. and trans. Benjamin Keen. New Brunswick, N.J.: Rutgers University Press, 1963.

Index